GOD HAS A PLAN FOR

CHURCH GOVERNMENT

*For I know the plans I have for you," declares the LORD, "plans to prosper you and not to harm you, plans to give you hope and a future.
Jeremiah 29:11*

By David Lange

GOD HAS A PLAN FOR THE CHURCH
CHURCH GOVERNMENT
By David E. Lange

Copyright © 2014 David E. Lange

All rights reserved. No portion of this book may be reproduced, stored in a retrieval system, or transmitted in any form or by any means—electronic, mechanical, photocopy, recording, scanning, or other—except for brief quotations in critical reviews or articles, without the prior written permission of the publisher.

Unless otherwise indicated, Scripture quotations are taken from the HOLY BIBLE: NEW INTERNATIONAL VERSION®. © 1973, 1978, 1984 International Bible Society. Used by permission of Zondervan. All rights reserved.

Scripture quotations marked NLT are taken from the *Holy Bible,* New Living Translation, copyright 1996, 2004. Used by permission of Tyndale House Publishers, Inc., Wheaton, Illinois 60189. All rights reserved.

Published by Lange Publishing, Pacific, MO
Library of Congress Control Number: 2014911674
ISBN 978-0-9824070-4-2
ISBN 0-9824070-4-1
Printed in the United States of America

This book is dedicated to . . .

Christy. She is my wonderful, supportive, and beautiful wife. Without the support of her and my awesome kids, Jeremiah, Bethany, Sofia, Bentley, and Blake this work would not have been possible.

Dad and Mom. I cherish the godly parents that I have been blessed with.

Mission Community Church. I also want to acknowledge and thank our church family for putting up with me during this process.

Debra. My very supportive sister, her family, Jon Marc, Nathan, Micah, and Natalie.

Of course the greatest honor and glory goes to Jesus Christ, my Lord and Savior!

For more information check out
WWW.BIBLEISTHEROCK.COM

If you were blessed by this series check out
WWW.FIVECOMMITMENTS.COM

CONTENTS

MUST READ INTRODUCTION — 1

TEN CHURCH GOVERNMENT LIFE TRUTHS — 9

CHURCH GOVERNMENT 1
THE CHURCH IS GOD'S DESIGN — 13

CHURCH GOVERNMENT 2
THE CHURCH PRAYS — 32

CHURCH GOVERNMENT 3
THE CHURCH HONORS THE SABBATH — 56

CHURCH GOVERNMENT 4
HONOR GOD WITH TITHES AND OFFERINGS — 90

CHURCH GOVERNMENT 5
THE CHURCH IS A FAMILY — 114

CHURCH GOVERNMENT 6
THE CHURCH IS AGAINST ABORTION — 141

CHURCH GOVERNMENT 7
THE CHURCH HONORS MARRIAGE — 165

CHURCH GOVERNMENT 8
THE CHURCH IS AGAINST GAMBLING — 191

CHURCH GOVERNMENT 9
THE CHURCH SUFFERS FOR CHRIST — 214

CHURCH GOVERNMENT 10
PREPARE FOR CHRIST'S RETURN — 236

MUST READ INTRODUCTION: GOD HAS A PLAN

God loves you. He created you. He longs for you to get to know Him better and to walk in His ways. God's love includes a plan for you, your family, the church, and the nation. He fully describes His plan in the Bible.

God's Word warns us about consequences that will occur when a nation turns away from Him. How do you think America is doing? Are we better off today? Are we worse off? The evidence is clear. We are experiencing some of God's consequences right now.

CONSEQUENCES FOR TURNING AWAY FROM GOD AND HIS WORD

- Debt - Deuteronomy 28:44
- More natural disasters – Deuteronomy 28:22-24; 2 Chronicles 7:13
- Losing God's protection – Deuteronomy 28:25
- A far away nation whose language we do not understand will come against us - Deuteronomy 28:49-50

President Andrew Jackson said, **"The Bible is the rock on which our republic rests."** This was true when our nation began, but it is no longer true today.

Today we have removed prayer, the Ten Commandments, and the Bible from our schools. Our families no longer devote time to studying Scripture and to following God's truths and principles.

People believe the lie that the founders wanted a separation of church and state. This lie distorts the meaning of the first amendment. It claims that having God in our schools breaks this amendment. But if this was true, would the authors and founders of the first amendment have had the Bible as the main textbook in their public schools? For four centuries, American families have cherished the Bible. They have believed it to be the rock on which this republic should rest.

In 1647, the first law for public education in America was called, "The Old Deluder Satan Act." The law declared, *"It being one chief project of that old deluder, Satan, to keep men from the knowledge of the Scriptures, as in former time…* Satan's goal is to keep men from the Holy Scriptures because God's Word is what leads people to a saving faith in Christ. Teaching Christianity is the best safeguard for any nation. To remove the teachings of Christ and His Word is to destroy a nation.

Societies of men must be governed in one way or another. They can either be governed with a heavy hand from a civil government or they can be self-governed based upon the teachings of Christ.

Heavy-handed government cannot restrain the sinfulness of man. Christ and Christ alone can change the character of man.

The foundation of Christ and His Word is what keeps a nation free. Do you think our nation is better off after removing God from our public schools? Are we less greedy, violent, or depressed? Are we more financially stable? Are our families more unified and loving or more separated and torn apart? America is suffering because we have taken God out of our lives. We need to repent and accept His perfect plan today.

Our country doesn't have to be this way. We can change the direction of this nation if we repent. Our founders knew this. They stood up and made a declaration to the world that they believed in a Creator. They understood that God had given them unalienable rights to be free and to worship Him as they pleased.

Do you believe the same? Are you willing to stand up for what you believe? Are you willing to cherish the Bible and begin studying it to find out what God's plan is for you, your family, the church, and our nation?

The four books in this series cover God's four ordained institutions: Self-Government / Family Government / Church Government / Civil Government.

They describe ten Life Truths for each institution. Each chapter presents a different Life Truth; a foundation for returning to God and for putting Him and His Word first in your life. Make a commitment to memorize these Life Truths as you work through the chapters.

CONSENT OF THE GOVERNED – ONE FAMILY AT A TIME

Our republic is still based upon the consent of the people. We are a government of the people, by the people, and for the people. As you return to God, and begin fulfilling the purposes God has for you in each of these institutions, seek to recruit others. Pray for our nation. Reach out to others in the hope that God will open their eyes and see the importance of obeying Him.

GOALS TO PRAY FOR:

- Individuals and families to return to studying, memorizing, and obeying God's Word
- Public schools to make the Bible the main textbook again
- The Ten Commandments to be obeyed and taught in our nation

ENGAGE PEOPLE WITH QUESTIONS LIKE THESE:

- Do you know that God has a plan for you, your family, the church, and our nation?
- Do you think our nation is headed in the right direction?
- Do you think our nation is more violent? More greedy?
- Do you think it was a good idea that we removed God and the Ten Commandments from our schools?
- Do you know God's Word says there will be consequences if we turn away from Him? *(Debt, loss of His protection, attacks from a nation from far away whose language we do not understand, more natural disasters)*
- Do you know that God will bless us if we turn back to Him?

FOLLOW UP WITH THIS QUESTION:

- Would you be interested in a Bible Study to learn more about God's plan for you, your family, the church, and our nation?

God allows suffering when we choose to turn away from Him. God promises blessings when we return to Him. Let's return to God and encourage everyone to do the same.

A PLAN OF ACTION FOR YOU, YOUR FAMILY, AND YOUR COMMUNITY:

1. Study and memorize the Life Truths for each institution.
2. Encourage others to join you (door to door, work, family, newspaper, etc…)
3. Encourage others to pray about running for a public office (school board, superintendent, alderman, mayor, etc…)
4. Begin a Facebook page or any other type of social media that will keep people informed (Have your goals clearly marked: We believe in God, the Apostles Creed, the Bible as the rock on which this nation rests, etc…) –This will help alert people to show up at City Hall for a vote or to voice their opinions.
5. Vote for Biblical laws. (Ex: a return to teaching the Bible in public schools)
6. **Direct people to the website *www.bibleistherock.com* for more information.**

A CHALLENGE FOR TODAY

Our founders understood the importance of knowing and heeding God's Word for future posterity. They also understood that godly leaders would need to be trained in the Bible. The first schools in our nation made sure that students got a Biblical education so they could lead with God's Word being the source for all law.

If we are going to have godly laws that lead us in righteousness, then we are going to need men and women who are willing to be the lawmakers. Who do we want in office making the laws that govern our nation? **Men and women who are God-fearing and who know the Bible well.**

For this to happen, "Christian" schools must make it a priority in their curriculum to raise up such leaders and prepare them for public offices. Not only do our "Christian" schools need to step up and refocus some of their goals, but we as a people need to engage more on a local level. We need to be willing to serve as mayors, aldermen, superintendents, and local school board members.

We must return to God so that He can forgive our sin and heal our land. We need to have a confidence and boldness to speak up for what we believe in. We need to study God's Word and teach all who will listen.

If we pray, study God's Word, obey Him, and spread the gospel, then we will be blessed by Him. God will hear our prayers, forgive our sins, and heal America again.

This is not an exhaustive study on the institutions just a starter guide to help us get things back into God's perfect order. *"His will being done on earth as it is in heaven."*

Read all four books and learn God's plan for the institutions.

Book 1 *God has a plan for you*
Self-Government

Book 2 *God has a plan for your family*
Family Government

Book 3 *God has a plan for the church*
Church Government

Book 4 *God has a plan for our nation*
Civil Government

**May God bless you and
may God bless our nation!**

TEN CHURCH GOVERNMENT LIFE TRUTHS

1. THE CHURCH IS GOD'S DESIGN

Question: What is God's design for the church?
Answer: The church is to be built upon the foundation of Christ.

John 14:6 (NIV) [6] Jesus answered, "I am the way and the truth and the life. No one comes to the Father except through me.

2. THE CHURCH PRAYS

Question: How should the church view prayer?
Answer: The church should always pray and not give up.

Luke 18:1 (NIV) [1] Then Jesus told his disciples a parable to show them that they should always pray and not give up.

3. THE CHURCH HONORS THE SABBATH

Question: How should the church view the Sabbath?
Answer: The church should rest on the Sabbath in obedience to the command.

Luke 23:56 (NIV) ⁵⁶ *Then they went home and prepared spices and perfumes. But they rested on the Sabbath in obedience to the commandment.*

4. THE CHURCH HONORS GOD WITH THEIR TITHES AND OFFERINGS

Question: How should the church view their tithes and offerings?
Answer: The church should honor God by bringing in their tithes and offerings.

Proverbs 3:9-10 (NIV) ⁹ *Honor the LORD with your wealth, with the firstfruits of all your crops;* ¹⁰ *then your barns will be filled to overflowing, and your vats will brim over with new wine.*

5. THE CHURCH IS A FAMILY

Question: How should the church view its members?
Answer: We should accept one another as God accepts us.

Matthew 12:49-50 (NIV) ⁴⁹ *Pointing to his disciples, he said, "Here are my mother and my brothers.* ⁵⁰ *For whoever does the will of my Father in heaven is my brother and sister and mother."*

6. THE CHURCH IS AGAINST ABORTION

Question: How should the church view life?
Answer: Every life is sacred and God chooses where and when a person is to be born.

Acts 17:26 (NIV) [26] *From one man he made every nation of men, that they should inhabit the whole earth; and he determined the times set for them and the exact places where they should live.*

7. THE CHURCH HONORS MARRIAGE

Question: How should the church view marriage?
Answer: Marriage is a sacred institution that God expects us to honor.

Hebrews 13:4 (NIV) [4] *Marriage should be honored by all, and the marriage bed kept pure, for God will judge the adulterer and all the sexually immoral.*

8. THE CHURCH IS AGAINST GAMBLING

Question: How should the church view gambling?
Answer: Gambling is the sin of greed and there should not be even a hint of greed in a Christian's life.

Ephesians 5:3 (NIV) [3] *But among you there must not be even a hint of sexual immorality, or of any kind of impurity, or of greed, because these are improper for God's holy people.*

9. THE CHURCH SUFFERS FOR CHRIST

Question: How should the church view suffering?
Answer: God uses sufferings to mold us and we will suffer for Christ on this earth.

Philippians 1:29 (NIV) [29] For it has been granted to you on behalf of Christ not only to believe on him, but also to suffer for him,

10. THE CHURCH PREPARES FOR CHRIST'S RETURN

Question: How should the church prepare for Christ's return?
Answer: The church should always be ready for no one knows the day or the hour of Christ's return.

Matthew 24:44 (NIV) [44] So you also must be ready, because the Son of Man will come at an hour when you do not expect him.

CHURCH GOVERNMENT
LIFE TRUTH # 1
THE CHURCH IS GOD'S DESIGN

The church is the third institution that God designed. God began with Self-Government when He created man. Then He established Family Government when He performed the first wedding ceremony of Adam and Eve. Now we are looking at Church Government.

Jesus established the church when He spoke to Peter and the apostles. He said in *Matthew 16:18 (NIV)* *[18] And I tell you that you are Peter, and on this rock **I will build my church**, and the gates of Hades will not overcome it.*

The church is not man's idea, just as Self and Family Government are not man's idea. Jesus came to establish the church and to teach us the responsibilities of the church. Jesus also said that, *"...the gates of Hades will not overcome the church."* The gates of Hades can also be translated the gates of hell. No matter how hard Satan tries to destroy the it, the church will always remain. Satan will never overcome the church.

This does not mean that the church will not suffer and go through hardships; but it does mean that it will never be overcome! Many times the church experiences the consequences of their own disobedience. The church also experiences tests from God regarding it's faithfulness. Throughout history there have been terrible persecutions against the church but the church has always overcome. Even in our generation, there are persecutions against Christians, but the church will never fall. The church is made up of believers. It is not the building. The word "church" comes from the Greek word *ekklesia* which is defined as "an assembly" or "called-out ones." We may say that we attend a certain church and refer to a building, but the Biblical church is not a building. It's the people who comprise the membership. The church is a group of born-again believers. In the New Testament, we see that these believers, many times, did not even have a building for worship. *Romans 16:5 (NIV) ⁵ Greet also the church that meets at their house.* When scripture speaks of a certain town, it refers to the people as the church. *I Corinthians 1:2 (NIV) ² To the church of God in Corinth.*

The Scriptures refer to a universal church and a local church. The universal church is comprised of all of those who have repented and made Jesus their Lord. Every believer from the beginning of creation, until the Lord establishes His kingdom, is included in the universal church. We will all be in heaven together. No matter what local church we attend; we are all united together in Christ. This passage refers to the local church and the universal church. *I Corinthians 1:2 (NIV) ² To the church of God in Corinth, to those sanctified in Christ Jesus and called to be holy, together with all those everywhere who call on the name of our Lord Jesus Christ–their Lord and ours:*

"In Corinth" refers to the local church and "all those everywhere" refers to the universal church. We probably know the members of our local church, but we are also members of a much bigger church. In heaven, we will get to know the universal church; believers in the Scriptures like Abraham, King David, Job, Peter, and Paul, to the people across the globe in our generation. One day we will all be in heaven together as the universal church.

There are many "titles" that refer to the church in the Scriptures. Here are a few: Body of Christ, Bride of Christ, New Creations, Saints, Household of God, and the Faithful. Titles that refer to the church are to be attributes of our character and symbolize the intimate relationship that we are to have with Christ. The Scriptures reveal an invisible church that cannot be seen by the naked eye. Jesus told parables that speak of the invisible church when He talked about the wheat and the tares and the sheep and the goats. What is meant by an invisible church? One day Jesus will return and judge all of the people. There are people on a church membership roll or who attend a church somewhere, who are not a part of Christ's church. Jesus told parables that illustrate the difference between those who really know Christ and those who just attend a worship service.

Matthew 25:32-33 (NIV) ³² All the nations will be gathered before him, and he will separate the people one from another as a shepherd separates the sheep from the goats. ³³ He will put the sheep on his right and the goats on his left.

The parable of the sheep and the goats reveals that only those who obey the teachings and follow the example of Christ will be a part of the invisible church. Although both the sheep and the goats call Him Lord, only the sheep truly know Him. This is what the goats say in *Matthew 25:44 (NIV) ⁴⁴ "They also will answer, 'Lord, when did we see you hungry or thirsty or a stranger or needing clothes or sick or in prison, and did not help you?'* On the Day of Judgment, the invisible church will become visible to all. It is so important for each of us to bend our knee to Jesus as Lord and seek to obey Him in all things.

The order of the church

1. Christ is the head of the Church

When Jesus established the church, He established it with order and structure. The church has leaders just as the family has leaders. Fathers are the head of the home. Christ is the head of the church. *Ephesians 5:23 (NIV) ²³ For the husband is the head of the wife as Christ is the head of the church, his body, of which he is the Savior.*

Christ is the foundation of the church. *Ephesians 1:22-23 (NIV) ²² And God placed all things under his feet and appointed him **to be head over everything for the church**, ²³ which is his body, the fullness of him who fills everything in every way.* The Bible reveals this symbolism of a foundation when it calls Christ the "chief cornerstone."

Ephesians 2:19-22 (NIV) ¹⁹ Consequently, you are no longer foreigners and aliens, but fellow citizens with God's people and members of God's household, ²⁰ built on the foundation of the apostles and prophets, with Christ Jesus himself as the chief cornerstone. ²¹ In him the whole building is joined together and rises to become a holy temple in the Lord. ²² And in him you too are being built together to become a dwelling in which God lives by his Spirit.

2. Membership

The Biblical church is exclusive in its membership. In our generation, we are being taught that there are many ways to heaven. Some claim that "all religions lead to the same god." Whether you attend a Mormon, Jehovah Witness, Islam, or other religious church, the popular view today is that everyone goes to heaven. This is completely false according to the Scriptures.

Look at this passage in *Colossians 1:15-22 (NIV) ¹⁵ He is the image of the invisible God, the firstborn over all creation. ¹⁶ For by him all things were created: things in heaven and on earth, visible and invisible, whether thrones or powers or rulers or authorities; all things were created by him and for him. [17] He is before all things, and in him all things hold together. [18] And he is the head of the body, the church; he is the beginning and the firstborn from among the dead, so that in everything he might have the supremacy. [19] For God was pleased to have all his fullness dwell in him, [20] and through him to reconcile to himself all things, whether things on earth or things in heaven, by making peace through his blood, shed on the cross. [21] Once you were alienated from God and were enemies in your minds because of your evil behavior. [22] But now he has reconciled you by Christ's physical body through death to present you holy in his sight, without blemish and free from accusation—*

This passage refers to the deity of Christ. Christ is God and as the passage states, *"in him all things hold together."* To accept another religion as true is to deny the truth of the Holy Scriptures. We are reconciled to God through the death of Christ's physical body on the cross. We are not reconciled through Buddha, Muhammad, Confucius, Joseph Smith, or any other leader who claims to know the way. The difference with Christianity, from every other religion, is that Christ ultimately defeated death.

One of the most exclusive statements that Jesus said about salvation is in *John 14:6 (NIV)* [6] *Jesus answered, "I am the way and the truth and the life. No one comes to the Father except through me."*

The passage in Colossians reveals to us how we can be reconciled to God and made holy. This is only possible because of Christ's physical death on the cross for our sins. Christ became sin for us so that we might become the righteousness of God. No other religion has a savior who paid for sin. We cannot be good enough to wash away our sin. Membership in Christ's church is exclusive because Jesus is the only way to get in. It is also inclusive because everyone is welcome to make Jesus their Lord and to be saved from their sins. *John 3:15-16 (NIV) [15] that everyone who believes in him may have eternal life. [16] "For God so loved the world that he gave his one and only Son, that whoever believes in him shall not perish but have eternal life."*

Romans 10:9 (NIV) [9] "That if you confess with your mouth," Jesus is Lord, "and believe in your heart that God raised him from the dead, you will be saved."

3. Leadership

The leadership of the church is centered around Christ and His Word. Christ is the head of the church. It is His Word that governs it. Our first Self-Government Life Truth taught us that Scripture alone governs us. Everything that the church does should be based upon Biblical principles found in the New Testament. This does not exclude Old Testament writings, however, Christ's life fulfilled many Old Testament requirements that the nation of

Israel faced. Look at the context of the passage when Jesus established the church:

Matthew 16:13-24 (NIV) [13] When Jesus came to the region of Caesarea Philippi, he asked his disciples, "Who do people say the Son of Man is?" [14] They replied, "Some say John the Baptist; others say Elijah; and still others, Jeremiah or one of the prophets." [15] "But what about you?" he asked. "Who do you say I am?" [16] Simon Peter answered, "You are the Christ, the Son of the living God." [17] Jesus replied, "Blessed are you, Simon son of Jonah, for this was not revealed to you by man, but by my Father in heaven. This first part of the passage reveals to us the exclusive way into membership into the church. It is dependent upon who we believe Jesus to be. Peter exclaims, "You are the Christ." The word Christ is a title and not a last name of Jesus. It means Messiah. Messiah refers to God's anointed; the One who the Old Testament foretold would come to be the King and would save the world from their sins.

Many have agreed that Jesus was a good teacher and a good moral leader. But they have failed to see the truth. The truth is that Jesus is the Christ. Jesus is God's anointed one. Jesus is God in the flesh. Jesus established the church. [18] *And I tell you that you are Peter, and on this rock I will build my church, and the gates of Hades will not overcome it.* The name Peter or Cephas means rock. Jesus is saying, *"You are called rock,"* and then he says, *"and on this rock I will build my church."*

I believe that Jesus was pointing to himself when He said, *"and on this rock."* Some believe that Jesus was referring to Peter as being the rock the church was founded upon. I disagree with this conclusion. Just a few verses later Jesus is saying to Peter. [22] *Peter took him aside and began to rebuke him. "Never, Lord!" he said. "This shall never happen to you!"* [23] *Jesus turned and said to Peter, "Get behind me, Satan! You are a stumbling block to me; you do not have in mind the things of God, but the things of men."* If Peter is the rock, then we are in trouble, because Peter is a man just like you in me. A few chapters later, Peter even denies Christ three times.

The church is not established by men because all men have sinned. The foundation of the church is Christ, the chief cornerstone! After Jesus told the disciples that He was going to build His church, He said, [19] *I will give you the keys of the kingdom of heaven; whatever you bind on earth will be bound in heaven, and whatever you loose on earth will be loosed in heaven."* Christ will give us the keys to the kingdom, not Peter or any other man. Christ himself will give us the keys and will build His church. Remember what Jesus said to Peter about being the Christ. Jesus said, *"Blessed are you, Simon son of Jonah, for this was not revealed to you by man, but by my Father in heaven."* The Holy Spirit gave Peter a key to the kingdom of heaven. Peter spoke about what the Holy Spirit had revealed to Him.

The keys to the kingdom come from God. They can be spoken through man, but they originate from God. No man is infallible. Only God himself. The church must keep it's foundation upon the Word of God and base everything it does on Scripture. God's Word must be what governs the church.

The church was built upon Christ, the prophets, and the apostles. *Ephesians 2:20 (NIV) [20] built on the foundation of the apostles and prophets, with Christ Jesus himself as the chief cornerstone.* The establishment of the church in a community is through the leadership of the church. The apostles went out and established elders and deacons to lead in the churches they started. *Titus 1:5 NIV) [5] The reason I left you in Crete was that you might straighten out what was left unfinished and appoint elders in every town, as I directed you.*

The church is to be established in a community by orderly and godly leadership. The congregation of the church is to submit to their leaders and become a light in the community. *Hebrews 13:17 (NIV) [17] Obey your leaders and submit to their authority. They keep watch over you as men who must give an account. Obey them so that their work will be a joy, not a burden, for that would be of no advantage to you.*

The congregation is also to test what is being said with the Word of God. *I John 4:1 (NIV) [1] Dear friends, do not believe every spirit, but test the*

spirits to see whether they are from God, because many false prophets have gone out into the world.
The church as a whole is to submit to God and the leadership of the local body. *Ephesians 5:24 (NIV) [24] Now as the church submits to Christ...*

The purpose of the church

Even though there is no specific verse that says, *"This is the purpose of the church,"* we know that the church was established to proclaim Jesus Christ as Lord and to submit to His reign in our lives. There are many things that the church is responsible to do, but **the main emphasis is to make Jesus Lord and follow in His footsteps.**

In the book of Acts, we get a glimpse of how powerful the church can be when we make Jesus our Lord. We need to seek to follow the lead of these early believers. Here is a good passage that sums up the early church. *Acts 2:42-47 (NIV) [42] They devoted themselves to the apostles' teaching and to the fellowship, to the breaking of bread and to prayer. [43] Everyone was filled with awe, and many wonders and miraculous signs were done by the apostles. [44] All the believers were together and had everything in common. [45] Selling their possessions and goods, they gave to anyone as he had need. [46] Every day they continued to meet together in the temple courts. They broke bread in their homes and ate together with glad and sincere hearts, [47] praising God and enjoying the favor of all the people. And the Lord added to their number daily those who were being saved.*

The early church devoted themselves to the teachings of Christ through the apostles. To devote means to commit by a solemn act. They devoted themselves to obey what God said. They devoted themselves to the fellowship of believers. They took the Lord's Supper together. They prayed together. They were committed to helping their neighbors and sacrificed so that everyone's needs could be met. They praised God and enjoyed the favor of all the people. To enjoy the favor means that they were unified and they loved each other deeply. They were so equipped by the apostles that they were evangelizing the lost and sharing with others the joy that they had found in Christ!

Wow! What a picture of how the church should be today! Lord Jesus, send a revival in our hearts that we would be servants for you and to one another just like the early church.

God desires to show His love and power through the church.

When Christ rose from the dead, He defeated death and hell. He made a way for God to dwell in man. This is what the New Testament called a mystery. It was kept hidden in the past, but is finally revealed in the New Testament. Look at what Paul says in *Colossians 1:24-27 (NIV) [24] Now I rejoice in what was suffered for you, and I fill up in my flesh what is still lacking in regard to Christ's afflictions, for the sake of his body, which is the church. [25] I have become its servant by the commission God gave me to present to you the word of God in its fullness—* [26] *the mystery that has been kept hidden for ages and generations, but is now disclosed to the saints.* [27] *To them God has chosen to make known among the Gentiles* **the glorious riches of this mystery, which is Christ in you, the hope of glory.**

The glorious riches of this mystery is that Christ can live in us! We can overcome our sinful natures and become like Christ. The Spirit of God Almighty can dwell in us and unify the church. We become one in Christ because of Christ in us!

Look at the prayer of Jesus for all believers in *John 17:20-23 (NIV)* [20] *"My prayer is not for them alone. I pray also for those who will believe in me through their message,* [21] *that all of them may be one, Father, just as you are in me and I am in you. May they also be in us so that the world may believe that you have sent me.* [22] *I have given them the glory that you gave me, that they may be one as we are one:* [23] *I in them and you in me. May they be brought to complete unity to let the world know that you sent me and have loved them even as you have loved me.*

Look at this passage in *Ephesians 3:10-11 (NIV)* [10] *His intent was that now, through the church, the manifold wisdom of God should be made known to the rulers and authorities in the heavenly realms,* [11] *according to his eternal purpose which he accomplished in Christ Jesus our Lord.*

God did some amazing things in the Old Testament, but now He desires to reveal to the rulers in the heavenly realms His power and might. God desires for the church to rise up and display His glory to the world. He has made a way to dwell in us and empower us to be free from sin.

*Luke 4:14-19 (NIV) ¹⁴ Jesus returned to Galilee in the power of the Spirit, and news about him spread through the whole countryside. ¹⁵ He taught in their synagogues, and everyone praised him. ¹⁶ He went to Nazareth, where he had been brought up, and on the Sabbath day he went into the synagogue, as was his custom. And he stood up to read. ¹⁷ The scroll of the prophet Isaiah was handed to him. Unrolling it, he found the place where it is written: ¹⁸ "The Spirit of the Lord is on me, because he has anointed me to preach good news to the poor. He has sent me **to proclaim freedom** for the prisoners and recovery of sight for the blind, to release the oppressed, ¹⁹ to proclaim the year of the Lord's favor."*

Jesus came and set people free from their addictions and their sins. He healed the sick, raised the dead, and set the captives free. Christ built His church to redeem the world and set people free.

Look at what Paul wrote in *I Corinthians 6:9-11 (NIV) ⁹ Do you not know that the wicked will not inherit the kingdom of God? Do not be deceived: Neither the sexually immoral nor idolaters nor adulterers nor male prostitutes nor homosexual offenders ¹⁰ nor thieves nor the greedy nor drunkards nor slanderers nor swindlers will inherit the kingdom of God. ¹¹ And that is what some of you were. But you were washed, you were sanctified, you were justified in the name of the Lord Jesus Christ and by the Spirit of our God.*

1. God desires to use us to help build His church.

The church is made up of the forgiven and the set free. Jesus spoke to an adulteress in the Gospel of John, Chapter 4. The Bible calls her the Samaritan woman. She was an outcast to the Jews and was living in sin. Jesus went to her and offered her living water. He offered her the choice to be forgiven of her sins and to be free from her immoral lifestyle. She accepted that Jesus was the Christ and she believed in Him. She not only believed in Him, but she went out and displayed the power of God to her town. *John 4:39 (NIV) ³⁹ Many of the Samaritans from that town believed in him because of the woman's testimony, "He told me everything I ever did."*

Christ came to proclaim freedom! The born-again are to proclaim freedom! The Apostle John says in *I John 1:2-3 (NIV) ² The life appeared; we have seen it and testify to it, and* **we proclaim to you the eternal life**, *which was with the Father and has appeared to us.* ³ **We proclaim to you** *what we have seen and heard, so that you also may have fellowship with us. And our fellowship is with the Father and with his Son, Jesus Christ.* When Christ forgives you and enters you, you are blown away by His love and power! So much so, that

you want to tell the whole world. This display of freedom from sin, joy, and boldness comes only through Christ in us, the hope of glory! This is a beautiful display of God's power! He can take a person who is basically dead and make them beautiful. He can take a wilted flower and make it beautiful again. He can take an ugly caterpillar and turn it into a beautiful butterfly. *2 Corinthians 5:17 (NIV) [17] Therefore, if anyone is in Christ, he is a new creation; the old has gone, the new has come!*
When we are born-again, God begins to unite us into local church bodies. We have a specific responsibility to spread our love for God and to tell the world how Christ has freed us from the power of sin. The forgiveness that Christ gives us clears our consciences and makes us bold witnesses for Him!

I hope that you are a part of the invisible church. I hope and pray that Christ is in you! I hope you have experienced the power of *Acts 3:19 (NIV) [19] Repent, then, and turn to God, so that your sins may be wiped out, that times of refreshing may come from the Lord,* Have you called on Jesus as your Lord and experienced your sins being wiped out? Have times of refreshing come from the Lord?

Church Government begins with Jesus Christ as Lord. He is the chief cornerstone!

WORKSHEET FOR CHURCH GOVERNMENT
LIFE TRUTH # 1
THE CHURCH IS GOD'S DESIGN

Question: What is God's design for the church?
Answer: The church is to be built upon the foundation of Christ.

John 14:6 (NIV) ⁶ Jesus answered, "I am the way and the truth and the life. No one comes to the Father except through me. Underline or highlight the verse. Write these corresponding verse references next to John 14:6; Romans 10:9-10; Colossians 1:15-20.

Write out the Life Truth, question, and answer on one side of an index card and the verse on the other side. Keep it in your Bible for the week. Work on it every day individually and as a family. Have it memorized by next week.

According to John 14:6 How is this passage exclusive?

Read John 3:15,16 How is this passage inclusive?

Read Colossians 1:13-20. According to verse 13, who is the "he" that Paul is referring to?

According to verse 16, who created all things?
In verse 17, how are all things held together?
In verse 18, who is the head of the church?
Who gets supremacy in all things?

In verse 20, who shed his blood on the cross so that we can be forgiven?

The main purpose of the church is to make Jesus the Lord of our lives. Read Ephesians 5:24. Who is the church supposed to submit to?
To submit is to yield to the governance and authority of another.

Read 1 John 2:6. How does this verse describe submitting?

Read Romans 8:5-9. According to verse 7, what cannot submit to God's law?

According to verse 9, how can we know that we are in Christ?

Read Romans 8:10-14. According to verse 10, if Christ is in us what is dead and what is alive?

In verse 11, the Spirit who did "what" is living in us?

In verse 12, what is our obligation?

In verse 13, what happens if we do not fulfill our obligation?

Read Romans 10:9,10. How can we be saved?

Based on this LIFE TRUTH, are you positive that Christ is living in you? Are there any areas in your life that you need to submit to the Lordship of Christ?

CHURCH-GOVERNMENT LIFE TRUTH # 2
THE CHURCH PRAYS

Prayer is communication between God and man. The Westminster Shorter Catechism says this about prayer, "an offering up of our desires unto God, for things agreeable to his will, in the name of Christ, with confession of our sins, and thankful acknowledgement of his mercies." From this statement, we realize that there is a lot to prayer. However, it is also so simple that even a child can pray.

The most amazing thing about prayer is that we can talk to Almighty God. We are all sinners and have broken God's law, but through His mercy He made a way for us to communicate with Him. This access of communication never has a busy signal and never asks us to leave a message. The prayer lines are always open and can handle billions of human beings praying at the same time with no delays. There is no limit to the amount of people who can access this line and still receive an answer from God.
There is no power failure, earthquake, lack of cell towers, flood, fire, or any other disaster that can interrupt the open prayer lines of God. David said this about the presence of God in *Psalm 139:7-12 (NIV)* [7] *Where can I go from your Spirit? Where can I flee from your presence?* [8] *If I go up to the heavens, you are there; if I make my bed in the depths, you are there.*

⁹ If I rise on the wings of the dawn, if I settle on the far side of the sea, ¹⁰ even there your hand will guide me, your right hand will hold me fast. ¹¹ If I say, "Surely the darkness will hide me and the light become night around me," ¹² even the darkness will not be dark to you; the night will shine like the day, for darkness is as light to you.

Not only are the prayer lines always open, but they take us right into the very throne room of God. The writer of Hebrews says this in *Hebrews 10:19-22 (NIV) ¹⁹ Therefore, brothers, since we have confidence to enter the Most Holy Place by the blood of Jesus, ²⁰ by a new and living way opened for us through the curtain, that is, his body, ²¹ and since we have a great priest over the house of God, ²² let us draw near to God with a sincere heart in full assurance of faith, having our hearts sprinkled to cleanse us from a guilty conscience and having our bodies washed with pure water.*

We have access to speak with God every second of the day with no delays. What an amazing opportunity for the people of God! This direct communication was made available to us by the blood of Jesus! Phone services costs monthly for limited minutes and even higher amounts for unlimited calls. How wonderful that Christ Jesus paid our bill for an all access direct line to God himself! If you were to call the president, pope, or any other leader, most likely you would never get through to speak to them. But those who know Jesus Christ as their Lord have all access availability at all times.

If there was one thing you could do to change the course of history and better our society would you do it? Prayer is a life changing experience for those who pray, as well as for those who are prayed for. Imagine what would happen in our nation and our communities if we took the power of prayer seriously.

Paul told us in *I Thessalonians 5:17 (NIV) [17] to pray continually*. How can we pray constantly? Do we have to be on our knees? Do we have to have our eyes closed? What does the passage *pray continually* mean?

Prayer does not have to be done on our knees or with our eyes closed. Prayer can be done anywhere and at any time. It can be individual or corporate. It can be out loud or silent. It can be while driving a car or in our homes. There is no limit to where or when we can pray. Therefore, it is possible to pray continually. We should always be praying about what the Lord wants us to do or how the Lord wants us to handle a situation.

The foundation of prayer rests on the fact that God desires to have a personal relationship with us. He wants to communicate with us. He is a personal being who desires to have fellowship with His children.

Prayer is not something that we naturally desire. Our fallen nature does not desire to communicate with God. It takes God intervening on our behalf for us to even desire to pray. God is at work in our lives; seeking to have a relationship with us. We need to call upon Him as Lord, confess our sins, and go to Him for help.

Prayer is a form of worship with many different aspects. We can confess our sins, give thanks to God, ask for wisdom, or intercede on behalf of another. These communications with God are all considered prayer. Prayer is a significant part of the spiritual life of a Christian. Look at what John said in *John 4:24 (NIV)* ^{24} *God is spirit, and his worshipers must worship in spirit and in truth.*

Several postures are listed in the Bible for praying; standing (Genesis 18:22); in bed (Psalm 63:5, 6); lying on the ground (Mark 14:35); kneeling (Acts 9:40); bowing (Psalm. 95:6, 7); praying with hands lifted up (Psalm. 28:2 and 1 Tim. 2:8). There is no set posture for prayer. However, we must come before our holy, all powerful God, with humility, reverence, and respect. God wants us to share our frustrations, confusion, anger, and questions; but we should always come before Him in reverence and awe.

BIBLICAL PRINCIPLES ON PRAYER

There are many examples and principles of prayer throughout Scripture. Hundreds of books have been published about prayer. This Life Truth, however, is not another detailed study on prayer. It has been written to encourage and remind Christians of their important responsibility to pray.

1. We must ask

The first principle is that we must ask. Look at what Jesus said in *Matthew 7:7-8 (NIV)* [7] *"Ask and it will be given to you; seek and you will find; knock and the door will be opened to you.* [8] *For everyone who asks receives; he who seeks finds; and to him who knocks, the door will be opened.*

God longs for us to pursue a relationship with Him. He loves to hear us ask Him for things. But because we know that God sees everything, we often feel unworthy to ask Him for anything. After all, we have sinned against Him. We have disobeyed. We have rebelled. We have deliberately gone our own way. We have sought to fulfill our own selfish desires over honoring Him. Why then would God want us to ask Him for anything?

BECAUSE HE LOVES US! How many parents have watched a child wander away and make horrible mistakes in life? How many of those parents would love for that child to turn around and say, *"Dad, Mom, I messed up. Will you help me?"* Most parents would jump at the chance to help their child. It wouldn't matter to them that the situation was brought on by their child's own bad choices.

The most important thing we need to understand is that we cannot make it without God. God longs for us to realize this and ask Him for help. He allows us to reap the consequences of our sin while He waits for us to pray to Him. When we pray to God, we are humbling ourselves to the fact that we need His help. It is an S.O.S call to our Savior and Lord. God says that we have not because we ask not.

2. Prayer allows us to do the improbable

Way too often I hear Christians say, *"I could never do that."* This statement might be true without a new spiritual nature from God. What if a man, who never got an education, came to Christ later in life? What if this man couldn't read or write and had struggled daily with communication? He may say, *"I can never learn to read or write."* But God's Word tells him differently. God's Word says that he can do anything with Christ.

Look at what Paul says in *Philippians 4:13 (NIV)* *¹³ I can do **everything** through him who gives me strength.* The word everything means exactly that. We can do everything with Christ in us. Jesus's brother said this in *James 1:5 (NIV) ⁵ If any of you lacks wisdom, he should ask God, **who gives generously to all** without finding fault, and it will be given to him.*

God will give wisdom and help you do anything you ask Him to do as long as it doesn't go against His will.

We are only responsible to humble ourselves and ask.

In the book of Exodus, we read about the life of Bezalel. Bezalel was a man who was unskilled as a craftsmen. One day, he had no skills. The next day he was an expert craftsman. The Bible says in *Exodus 31:1-6 (NIV)* [1] *Then the LORD said to Moses,* [2] *"See, I have chosen Bezalel son of Uri, the son of Hur, of the tribe of Judah,* [3] ***and I have filled him with the Spirit of God, with skill, ability and knowledge in all kinds of crafts--*** [4] *to make artistic designs for work in gold, silver and bronze,* [5] *to cut and set stones, to work in wood, and to engage in all kinds of craftsmanship.*
How did Bezalel become an expert craftsman? Did he go to school and study? Was he a journeyman first? Did he sit under the teachings of another? No, the Bible says the Spirit of God filled him and made him an expert craftsman. How do I know he was an expert? Because God never does anything halfway. This man was filled with the Spirit and was given the ability to build the temple.

If you need wisdom; ask for wisdom. If you need to be set free from an addiction; ask God to set you free. If you need your needs met; ask God to provide them. Look at the example that Jesus taught us in the Lord's Prayer. *Give us, forgive us, lead us.* We are to ask God for help.

God longs to give us more of himself. He wants to help us in this life. But we must ask Him. Look at the passage in *Luke 11:11-13 (NIV) ¹¹ "Which of you fathers, if your son asks for a fish, will give him a snake instead? ¹² Or if he asks for an egg, will give him a scorpion? ¹³ If you then, though you are evil, know how to give good gifts to your children,* **how much more will your Father in heaven give the Holy Spirit to those who ask him!"**

When we have God's Spirit in us, we are able to do so much more for the Glory of God. God gives to those who ask Him. Without His Spirit, we cannot walk in righteousness. Our flesh is unable to be righteous. We need God's Spirit in us. *Mark 14:38 (NIV) ³⁸* **Watch <u>and pray</u>** *so that you will not fall into temptation.* **The spirit is willing, but the body is weak**."

3. We need individual prayer and corporate prayer

a. Individual prayer

God wants to have a relationship with each and every one of us on an individual level. We all have specific needs, weaknesses, and sinful desires. God wants to help us individually. He wants to mold us into a Christ-likeness based upon our own issues. We have past issues that affect us. We have present pressures that pull at us. We have desires that arise in our thoughts. We have hurts, pains, and fears that Christ wants to help us with individually. We have the master physician who is willing to meet with us whenever we like. We don't have to make an advance appointment. We can go to Him anytime. There is no after-hour phone service that handles His calls. He is ready to deal with us individually whenever we call.

Look at what Jesus said in *Matthew 6:5-6 (NIV)* [5] *"And when you pray, do not be like the hypocrites, for they love to pray standing in the synagogues and on the street corners to be seen by men. I tell you the truth, they have received their reward in full.* [6] ***But when you pray, go into your room, close the door and pray to your Father, who is unseen. Then your Father, who sees what is done in secret, will reward you.*** God will reward those who go to him in prayer in secret. Christians need to have daily time with the Lord in prayer. Who doesn't want to be rewarded? Who doesn't need more of the Spirit? Who could use more of Christ's Spirit in them? Every single one of us. The fact that the church is in such a mess is evidence that many Christians are not praying to God in secret.

b. Corporate prayer

If you have read the book of Acts, then you know about the powerful birth of the Christian church. One thing that was constant in the life of the early church was their corporate prayer life. Look at what it says in *Acts 1:14 (NIV)* [14] *They all joined together* ***constantly*** *in prayer, along with the women and Mary the mother of Jesus, and with his brothers.* We have read about the miracles in the book of Acts. We have read about the thousands of people being born again. We have read about the healings and great boldness of the church. But have we ever noticed their commitment to prayer?

They were constantly devoting themselves to prayer. Look at this passage in *Acts 2:42 (NIV)* [42] **They devoted themselves** *to the apostles' teaching and to the fellowship, to the breaking of bread and* **to prayer.** The words *constantly* and *devoted* seem to be missing in the description of our current church prayer meetings. Many churches have canceled their once a week prayer meetings. Those who have continued such a service aren't necessarily devoted to it. The current statistics of those who attend a weekly prayer service versus those who attend church on Sunday morning are startling to say the least. Jesus expects us to come together and pray. He wants us to ask Him for strength and to lift up the issues in our community. We are to devote ourselves to prayer.

Jesus was so encouraged about the prayer life of the early church that on one occasion He shook the building. I believe that this was His way of saying, *"Way to go, great job! Thank you for allowing me to move in this situation."* Remember we have not, because we ask not. Look at what it says about the churches prayer in *Acts 4:29-31 (NIV)* [29] *Now, Lord, consider their threats and enable your servants to speak your word with great boldness.* [30] *Stretch out your hand to heal and perform miraculous signs and wonders through the name of your holy servant Jesus." ³¹* **After they prayed, the place where they were meeting was shaken. And they were all filled with the Holy Spirit and spoke the word of God boldly.** Not only did God shake the building, but He filled them with his Spirit. This enabled them to walk in boldness and righteousness.

The church needs to re-devote itself to individual prayer times and corporate prayer times. We need to stop being so busy with the things of this world and engage in the more important matter of prayer. Think about what could happen if we devoted ourselves to constantly praying together.

ANSWERED AND UNANSWERED PRAYER

1. Sin affects our prayers

If we are in defiant sin against God's will, He will not hear us. There are times when He lets us suffer the consequences of our sin. Until we repent, God will allow the trouble to come. Trouble and other daily issues in life are what God uses to discipline us unto righteousness. Look at what it says in *Isaiah 1:15-16 (NIV)*¹⁵ *When you spread out your hands in prayer, I will hide my eyes from you;* ***even if you offer many prayers, I will not listen.*** *Your hands are full of blood;* ¹⁶ *wash and make yourselves clean. Take your evil deeds out of my sight! Stop doing wrong,*

We must repent and confess our sins to God. We must seek to follow the example that Jesus left us on the earth. This is why our individual prayer times are so important. We need to be asking God to reveal to us anything that may be in rebellion to His will. He will reveal it to us in our secret place and give us the strength to overcome when we repent.

2. Obedience effects our prayers

Just as sin affects our prayers, obedience affects them as well. When we are obeying the commands of God, God is willing to answer our prayers. Many times we become comfortable in our "good" state, but God is calling us to holiness. God is longing for us to be like Jesus in all things. We are not to lessen the call of righteousness. We need to be on our knees asking God to transform us into being holy. The righteous have powerful and effective prayers. Have you noticed that the ability to be holy does not come from us? We are fallen beings. We must be on our knees, constantly asking God for the strength to walk in righteousness.

Look at what John says in *1 John 3:21-22 (NIV)*
²¹ Dear friends, if our hearts do not condemn us, we have confidence before God ²² **and receive from him anything we ask, because <u>we obey his commands and do what pleases him</u>.**

As we are walking with Christ and seeking to do what pleases Him, we are more concerned about His kingdom than our own. Therefore, as we pray we will be asking things in accordance to His will and not just for our own benefit. John puts it this way in *1 John 5:14-15 (NIV)* *[14] This is the confidence we have in approaching God: **that if we ask anything according to his will**, he hears us. [15] And if we know that he hears us—whatever we ask—**we know that we have what we asked of him.***

3. God's will can affect our prayers

There are times in life that God says no to our prayers. Paul was dealing with an affliction that tormented him. Paul says that he pleaded with God to remove this affliction, but God's will was that it remain. Look at what the passage states in *2 Corinthians 12:7-9 (NIV) [7] To keep me from becoming conceited because of these surpassingly great revelations, there was given me a thorn in my flesh, a messenger of Satan, to torment me. [8] Three times I pleaded with the Lord to take it away from me. [9] But he said to me, "My grace is sufficient for you, for my power is made perfect in weakness." Therefore I will boast all the more gladly about my weaknesses, so that Christ's power may rest on me.*

You may be going through a rough time like Paul. You may be wondering why God is allowing you to endure such a thing. God's will may not be to remove the affliction or remove you from the situation. But you can be assured that whatever God is allowing is for your own benefit. Even when God is chastising or testing you, it is for your benefit. He longs to mold you into the image of His son. Many times, you have to go through the fire to take out impurities. The promise that you can hold onto during these times is found in *Romans 8:28 (NIV)* *²⁸ And we know that **in all things** God works for the good of those who love him, who have been called according to his purpose. In* all things includes afflictions, tests, and persecutions.

God could have removed the affliction in Paul's life. The Lord knew that if He did, Paul would have become conceited. The affliction reminded Paul of his dependence on God and his frail position as a human. We need to thank God even for the "no" answers to our prayers.

4. Fasting can affect our prayers

Fasting is refraining from eating food. Some fasts involved refraining from food as well as water. A fast from food never lasted for more than 40 days. Food and water fasts never lasted for more than three days.

In Mark, Chapter 9, the disciples were unable to drive out an evil spirit that possessed a man's son. The father asked Jesus if he could drive out the evil spirit and Jesus said in *Mark 9:23 (NIV)* ²³ *"'If you can?" said Jesus. "Everything is possible for him who believes."* Jesus healed the boy and commanded the evil spirit to come out and never enter him again. Afterwards

the disciples asked Jesus in *Mark 9:28-29 (NIV)*
28 After Jesus had gone indoors, his disciples asked him privately, "Why couldn't we drive it out?" 29 He replied, "This kind can come out only by prayer and fasting."
We know that Jesus wants us to fast. He told us to fast in the Sermon on the Mount when he said in *Matthew 6:16-18 (NIV)* *16* **"When you fast***, do not look somber as the hypocrites do, for they disfigure their faces to show men they are fasting. I tell you the truth, they have received their reward in full. 17* **But when you fast***, put oil on your head and wash your face, 18 so that it will not be obvious to men that you are fasting, but only to your Father, who is unseen; and your Father, who sees what is done in secret, will reward you.*

The early church continued the practice of fasting. It says in *Acts 13:2-3 (NIV)* *2 While they were worshiping the Lord and* **fasting***, the Holy Spirit said, "Set apart for me Barnabas and Saul for the work to which I have called them." 3* **So after they had fasted and prayed***, they placed their hands on them and sent them off.*
Acts 14:23 (NIV) *23 Paul and Barnabas appointed elders for them in each church and,* **with prayer and fasting***, committed them to the Lord, in whom they had put their trust.*

We have evidence that some things cannot get accomplished through prayer alone. Sometimes Jesus wants us to fast and pray.

JESUS' EXAMPLE OF PRAYER

These five passages reveal the example that Jesus left us in prayer.

Luke 5:16 (NIV) ¹⁶ *But Jesus **often** withdrew to lonely places and prayed.*

Luke 6:12 (NIV) ¹² *One of those days Jesus went out to a mountainside to pray, and spent the night praying to God.*

Matthew 14:23 (NIV) ²³ *After he had dismissed them, he went up on a mountainside by himself to pray. When evening came, he was there alone.*

Mark 1:35 (NIV) ³⁵ *Very early in the morning, while it was still dark, Jesus got up, left the house and went off to a solitary place, where he prayed.*

Hebrews 5:7 (NIV) ⁷ *During the days of Jesus' life on earth, he offered up prayers and petitions with loud cries and tears to the one who could save him from death, and he was heard because of his reverent submission.*

Jesus came to show us how to live. It is important for us to follow His lead. His prayer life was noticed by his disciples. They asked Him to teach them how to pray. The disciples saw the power that came from His prayer times. They saw the renewed strength, boldness, and love that came from the secret times that Jesus had with God.

THERE IS POWER IN PRAYER

Jesus was very clear when He spoke about the power available to us in prayer. We must believe that God hears our prayers and answers them. We must walk in righteousness and cry out to God so He will move on our behalf for His Glory. Praying is a sign of humility. It shows that we need God to intervene on our behalf.

John 14:12-14 (NIV) [12] *I tell you the truth, anyone who has faith in me will do what I have been doing. He will do even greater things than these, because I am going to the Father.* [13] ***And I will do whatever you ask in my name,*** *so that the Son may bring glory to the Father.* [14] ***You may ask me for anything in my name, and I will do it.***

John 15:6-8 (NIV) [6] *If anyone does not remain in me, he is like a branch that is thrown away and withers; such branches are picked up, thrown into the fire and burned.* [7] ***If you remain in me and my words remain in you, ask whatever you wish, and it will be given you.*** [8] *This is to my Father's glory, that you bear much fruit, showing yourselves to be my disciples.*

Obedience and faith are the two key elements in having a powerful prayer life.

Obedience comes from our time in the Word; and grows from our private prayer lives.

Faith comes from our time in the Word; and grows by our being active in the church. The Holy Spirit gives us both obedience and faith. We need to ask God for the ability to live a righteous life and to increase our faith.

Look at this passage in James. It reveals the obedient righteous life and the faith necessary to pray.
James 5:13-16 (NIV) [13] *Is any one of you in trouble?* **He should pray.** *Is anyone happy? Let him sing songs of praise.* [14] *Is any one of you sick? He should call the elders of the church to pray over him and anoint him with oil in the name of the Lord.* [15] **And the prayer offered in faith will make the sick person well;** *the Lord will raise him up. If he has sinned, he will be forgiven.* [16] *Therefore confess your sins to each other and pray for each other so that you may be healed.* **The prayer of a righteous man is powerful and effective.**

Most of us could grow in our obedience and faith. Most of us do not have powerful prayer lives that allow us to see God move in mighty ways. Will we just shrug our shoulders and say, *"Oh, well"*? Or will we begin to devote ourselves to continually praying individually and corporately? If we devote ourselves to prayer, we will become more righteous and our faith will increase.

Our nation is in a mess. We need another spiritual awakening. The awakening will not come until the people of God repent and ask Him for help. We must intercede on behalf of our nation. We must come together as a church and lift up our leaders. *I Timothy 2:1-2 (NIV) ¹ I urge, then, first of all, that requests, prayers, intercession and thanksgiving be made for everyone— ² for kings and **all those in authority**, that we may live peaceful and quiet lives in all godliness and holiness.* What would happen if families and churches began to live righteous lives, increase their faith, and pray powerful prayers over our nation? Look at this passage in *Exodus 32:7-14 (NIV) ⁷ Then the LORD said to Moses, "Go down, because your people, whom you brought up out of Egypt, have become corrupt. ⁸ They have been quick to turn away from what I commanded them and have made themselves an idol cast in the shape of a calf. They have bowed down to it and sacrificed to it and have said, 'These are your gods, O Israel, who brought you up out of Egypt.' ⁹ "I have seen these people," the LORD said to Moses, "and they are a stiff-necked people. ¹⁰ Now leave me alone so that my anger may burn against them and that I may destroy them. Then I will make you into a great nation."*

The sin of the nation of Israel had grieved God so much so that He was ready to destroy them. When Moses was on the mountain getting the Ten Commandments, the people felt like it was taking way too long. They decided to take matters into their own hands and make a false god.

Could our nation be in a similar situation where God is fed up with our sins? What happened to the nation of Israel? Did God destroy their nation? Look at what Moses did:

[11] But Moses sought the favor of the LORD his God. "O LORD," he said, "why should your anger burn against your people, whom you brought out of Egypt with great power and a mighty hand? [12] Why should the Egyptians say, 'It was with evil intent that he brought them out, to kill them in the mountains and to wipe them off the face of the earth'? Turn from your fierce anger; relent and do not bring disaster on your people. [13] Remember your servants Abraham, Isaac and Israel, to whom you swore by your own self: 'I will make your descendants as numerous as the stars in the sky and I will give your descendants all this land I promised them, and it will be their inheritance forever.'" Moses boldly pleaded with God to not destroy the people. Moses reminded God of His call to make the nation into a powerful witness for His glory. Look at what verse 14 says after Moses interceded for the nation:

[14] Then the LORD relented and did not bring on his people the disaster he had threatened. It is our job as the church to intercede on behalf of our leaders and the sins of our people.

The church in America needs to wake up to the mission of constantly praying together so God can do His work in our families, our communities, and our nation. Earlier I asked, *"If there was one thing that you could do to change the course of history and better our society would you do it?"* and *"What could happen in our nation and communities if we understood and took the power of prayer seriously?"*

Prayer is one of the weapons that God has given us to push back the darkness in our society. When we do not pray, it's like trying to put out a forest fire with small buckets of water. God has given us the ability to call down the rain and put out the fires. All we need is to do is use the power of prayer.

WORKSHEET FOR CHURCH GOVERNMENT
LIFE TRUTH # 2
THE CHURCH PRAYS

Question: How should the church view prayer?
Answer: The church should always pray and not give up.
Luke 18:1 (NIV) ¹ Then Jesus told his disciples a parable to show them that they should always pray and not give up. Underline or highlight the verse. Write these corresponding verse references next to Luke 18:1 – Acts 1:14; 2:42

> Write out the Life Truth, question, and answer on one side of an index card and the verse on the other side. Keep it in your Bible for the week. Work on it every day individually and as a family. Have it memorized by next week.

Read Luke 18:1-8. According to verse 1, what is Jesus' main point of this parable?

What does Jesus mean when he says, *"Will he find faith on the earth?"*

Read Acts 1:14. How often did the church get together to pray?

Read Acts 2:42. What did the church devote themselves to? A_____ T_____,

F_____, B_____ of
B_____ and to P_____.

Read Luke 6:12-16. What was the big decision Jesus was praying about?

How long did he pray according to verse 12?

Read Luke 11:5-13. According to verse 8, what was it that caused the friend to help out?

According to verses 9,10 what will God do if we Ask, Seek, Knock?

Ask = _____

Seek = _____

Knock = _____

Read 1 John 3:21,22. Verse 22 says we receive because we O_____ H_____ C_____ and do what pleases him.

Read Acts 12:1-5. What was the church doing when Peter was arrested?

The Bible describes the kind of praying they were doing. They were E_____ praying.

Describe what earnestly might have looked like or not looked like.

Read Luke 5:16. What do we learn about Jesus' prayer life in this verse?

Read Numbers 11:1-3. What caused the fire to die down? (v2)

Read Romans 12:12. This passage tells us to be faithful in prayer. List one way that you could improve in your faithfulness.

Based on this LIFE TRUTH, what can you do individually and as a family to be more devoted to prayer?

CHURCH-GOVERNMENT LIFE TRUTH # 3
THE CHURCH HONORS THE SABBATH

The command to "keep the Sabbath holy" is no more than a suggestion in the church today. In fact, some preachers even say that honoring the Sabbath is not even taught in the New Testament. Other preachers teach that man needs a day of rest and suggest that Christians pick their own day. Was this the intent of Christ; that we choose our own day to rest? Or is there more to this rest than we seem to understand? In the Old Testament, the Sabbath was on Saturday, the last day of the week. God created the world and everything in it in six days. Then He rested on the seventh day. His resting on the seventh day from work became part of the creation order. The Sabbath Commandment states in *Exodus 20:11 (NIV) 11 For in six days the LORD made the heavens and the earth, the sea, and all that is in them, but he rested on the seventh day. Therefore the LORD blessed the Sabbath day and made it holy.*

The Sabbath has been around since creation. The LORD blessed it as a holy day. The Apostles, inspired by the Holy Spirit, moved the Sabbath from Saturday to Sunday in the New Testament. We see hints of this move in the New Testament and we see concrete evidence in history itself. Christian churches still meet today for worship on Sunday.

Why? Because this is the tradition passed down to us by the early church and the apostles.

Philip Schaff wrote a book called the History of the Christian Church Volume I. In it he said, "The LORD'S DAY (SUNDAY) took the place of the Jewish Sabbath (Saturday) as the weekly day of public worship. The substance remained, the form was changed. The institution of a periodical weekly day of rest for the body and the soul is rooted in our physical and moral nature, and is as old as man, dating, like marriage, from paradise." Phillip Schaff went on to say, "**The universal and un-contradicted Sunday observance in the second century can only be explained by the fact that it had its roots in apostolic practice.**"

Phillip Schaff said of the Sunday observance, "The due observance of it, (The Lord's Day) in which the churches of England, Scotland, and America, to their incalculable advantage, excel the churches of the European continent, is a wholesome school of discipline, a means of grace for the people, a safeguard of public morality and religion, a bulwark against infidelity, **and a source of immeasurable blessing to the church, the state, and the family. Next to the Church and the Bible, the Lord's Day is the chief pillar of Christian society.**"

Throughout history, until this generation, the Sabbath was considered a **"chief pillar of Christian** society" and a **"safeguard for public morality and religion."** Is this generation a pillar of morality? Perhaps, we need to reconsider our position on the Sabbath and the blessings associated with this Commandment. Is the moral decay of our society somehow tied to our disobedience to God's command to honor the Sabbath and keep it holy?

The pastors of our founding era felt that the observance of the Sabbath, as stated in the Ten Commandments, was as important to obey as the law to not steal. To neglect the Sabbath **would bring the destruction of a nation; for it is God who makes us holy, and it is He that blesses us for our obedience to His commands.**

THE SABBATH IS TO BE A DAY OF REST

Exodus 20:8-11 (NIV) [8] "Remember the Sabbath day by keeping it holy. [9] Six days you shall labor and do all your work, [10] but the seventh day is a Sabbath to the LORD your God. On it you shall not do any work, neither you, nor your son or daughter, nor your manservant or maidservant, nor your animals, nor the alien within your gates. [11] For in six days the LORD made the heavens and the earth, the sea, and all that is in them, but he rested on the seventh day. Therefore the LORD blessed the Sabbath day and made it holy.

THE SABBATH IS FOR CORPORATE WORSHIP

The Sabbath was made for corporate worship. We see this in the New Testament as the Jews would attend the synagogue together on the Sabbath. We are not meant to meet on our own or choose our own day to rest. We are to do it corporately. We who are many form one body and together we become the mighty army for God.

CAN THE SABBATH BE ANY DAY WE CHOOSE?

Romans 14:5,6 (NIV) ⁵ One man considers one day more sacred than another; another man considers every day alike. Each one should be fully convinced in his own mind. ⁶ He who regards one day as special, does so to the Lord. He who eats meat, eats to the Lord, for he gives thanks to God; and he who abstains, does so to the Lord and gives thanks to God.

We do not pick our own day to honor the Sabbath. The stipulations in the command are to work six days and then rest on the seventh. This passage in Romans was referring to the Jews who wanted to continue some of the Old Testament festivals they had grown up with; not for salvation purposes, but because they were still very meaningful to them. This happens today when we celebrate

December 25th as Jesus' birthday. December 25th is most likely not the day that Jesus was born. However, we still choose to celebrate this day to honor His birth. Paul is NOT saying to pick your own day to have a Sabbath. That view would be inconsistent with the New Testament teaching to have corporate worship.

THE CHURCH MEETS TOGETHER FOR WORSHIP AND INSTRUCTION

Mark 6:2 (NIV) ² When the Sabbath came, **he began to teach in the synagogue**, and many who heard him were amazed. *"Where did this man get these things?" they asked. "What's this wisdom that has been given him, that he even does miracles?"* When Jesus came on the scene, the Jewish people were meeting in synagogues for corporate worship on Saturdays.

The writer of Hebrews tells the believers to not give up meeting together. Hebrews 10:25 (NIV) ²⁵ *Let us not give up meeting together, as some are in the habit of doing, but let us encourage one another–and all the more as you see the Day approaching.* If we all picked our own Sabbath, some might meet on Monday, others Tuesday, and so on. This would not be meeting together as God intended.

Jesus refers to corporate worship in the Sermon on the Mount. He speaks of the altar in Matthew 5:23-24 (NIV) ²³ *"Therefore, if you are offering your gift at the altar and there remember that your brother has something against you, 24 leave your gift there in front of the altar. First go and be reconciled to your brother; then come and offer your gift.* When did the nation come to the altar? It was on Saturday. Their day of worship.

Many passages in the New Testament refer to Christians coming together. *I Corinthians 14:26 (NIV) 26 What then shall we say, brothers? When you come together, everyone has a hymn, or a word of instruction, a revelation, a tongue or an interpretation. All of these must be done for the strengthening of the church.* The Scriptures clearly teach corporate worship in the New Testament. It is not consistent with the Bible to assume that we can meet on any day we want.

THE CHURCH MEETS ON THE SAME DAY

Sometimes the church faces issues that need to be addressed. *Matthew 18:15-17 (NIV) 15 "If your brother sins against you, go and show him his fault, just between the two of you. If he listens to you, you have won your brother over. 16 But if he will not listen, take one or two others along, so that 'every matter may be established by the testimony of two or three witnesses.' 17 If he refuses to listen to them, tell it to the church; and if he refuses to listen even to the church, treat him as you would a pagan or a tax collector.* How could we tell it to the church if everyone was meeting on different days?

Notice these passages and their intent for us to come together on the same day. *I Corinthians 11:18 (NIV) [18] In the first place, I hear that **when you come together as a church**, there are divisions among you, and to some extent I believe it.*

*I Corinthians 11:20 (NIV) [20] **When you come together**, it is not the Lord's Supper you eat, Romans 12:4-5 (NIV) [4] Just as each of us has one body with many members, and these members do not all have the same function, [5] so in Christ we who are many form one body, and each member belongs to all the others.*

*I Corinthians 12:25-28 (NIV) [25] so that there should be no division in the body, but that its parts should have equal concern for each other. [26] If one part suffers, every part suffers with it; if one part is honored, every part rejoices with it. [27] **Now you are the body of Christ, and each one of you is a part of it.** [28] And in the church God has appointed first of all apostles, second prophets, third teachers, then workers of miracles, also those having gifts of healing, those able to help others, those with gifts of administration, and those speaking in different kinds of tongues.*

*Ephesians 4:11-13 (NIV) [11] It was he who gave some to be apostles, some to be prophets, some to be evangelists, and some to be pastors and teachers, [12] to prepare God's people for works of service, **so that the body of Christ may be built up** [13] until **we all reach unity in the faith** and in the knowledge of the Son of God and* *become mature, attaining to the whole measure of the fullness of Christ.*

*Ephesians 4:16 (NIV) ¹⁶ From him the **whole body**, joined and held together by every supporting ligament, grows and builds itself up in love, **as each part does its work.*** How can we reach unity and all do our part to minister to the body if we are not meeting together? The implication in Scripture is that we come together as the church.

*Acts 20:7 (NIV) ⁷ On the first day of the week **we came together** to break bread. Paul spoke to the people and because he intended to leave the next day, kept on talking until midnight.* The phrase to break bread means that they took the Lord's Supper together. We are to meet together corporately to take the Lord's Supper together as Christ commanded us to do. This is to be done corporately as a church body.

Those who read Romans 14 and conclude that Paul was referring to the ability to choose any day to worship as the Sabbath are denying the overall teaching in the New Testament that believers are to come together for corporate worship.

HOW DID THE FOUNDERS OF AMERICA VIEW THE SABBATH?

The founders were so concerned about this nation honoring the fourth commandment of the Ten Commandments that they established a law to help us obey it. The Blue Law was designed to enforce moral standards in America, particularly the observance of Sunday as a day of worship or rest. It also restricted Sunday shopping.

The law was changed in the 1980s. The first change stated that businesses would only be open during non-church hours and that no alcohol could be sold. Today, however, almost everything is open and alcohol can be sold. Sunday is now the second-busiest shopping day of the week. Would the founders be pleased with our decision to do away with the Blue Law? What would they think of the Sabbath being treated just like any other day of the week?

A book entitled Political Sermons of the American Founding Era, gives us a glimpse of what the founders believed was important to sustain our great nation. This country has experienced the blessings of their faith and commitment to God. It is now our responsibility to be just as diligent by passing the same blessings on to the generations after us. Unfortunately, we have gotten off course. Christians need to return to the Godly foundation our forefathers left for us.

In the book, Pastor Timothy Dwight said, **"To destroy us, therefore, in this dreadful sense, our enemies must first destroy our *Sabbath*, and seduce us from the house of God.** (Ellis Sandoz, *Political Sermons of the American Founding Era: 1730-1805*, 2 vols, Foreword by Ellis Sandoz (2nd ed.

Indianapolis: Liberty Fund, 1998). Vol. 2. Chapter: 48: Timothy Dwight, THE DUTY OF AMERICANS, AT THE PRESENT CRISIS)

One of the greatest tools that Satan uses in our generation to seduce us from the house of God involves our love for entertainment and sports. Today Christians often skip church to go and watch their favorite sports team. The founders felt so strongly about honoring the Sabbath that they enforced a law to protect it. Sunday used to be a day of moral instruction and was considered a chief pillar in a Christian society. Look at the moral decay in the world today and then think about how we treat the Sabbath with contempt. Perhaps, the founding fathers understood something that we are overlooking to our own destruction. These men would not have broken the Sabbath for any reason in their generation. They would have treated the day as God had intended; a day to worship God and rest.

Pastor Dwight goes on to say, "Among the particular duties required by this precept, and at the present time, **none holds a higher place than the observation of the Sabbath.** The Sabbath and its ordinances have ever been the great means of all moral good to mankind. The faithful observation of the Sabbath is, therefore, one of the chief duties and interests of men; but the present time furnishes reasons, peculiar, at least in degree, for exemplary regard to this divine institution. **The enemies of God have by private argument, ridicule, and influence, and by public decrees, pointed their**

especial malignity against the Sabbath; and have expected, and not without reason, that, if they could annihilate it, they should overthrow Christianity. From them we cannot but learn its importance. Enemies usually discern, with more sagacity, the most promising point of attack, than those who are to be attacked. In this point are they to be peculiarly opposed. Here, peculiarly, are their designs to be baffled. If they fail here, they will finally fail. **Christianity cannot fall, but by the neglect of the Sabbath.**

Pastor Joseph Sewall wrote a sermon called Nineveh's Repentance and Deliverance. In it he states, "Do your utmost that the worship of God may be maintain'd in the power and purity of it, among this people. Let all due care be taken that men may fear this *glorious and fearful name*, the Lord our God, and not presume to take it in vain; for *because of swearing the land mourns*. **Let the Lord's-day be strictly observ'd; for God hath set the *Sabbath* as a sign between him and his people, that he is the Lord who sanctifieth them.** (Ellis Sandoz, *Political Sermons of the American Founding Era: 1730-1805*, 2 vols, Foreword by Ellis Sandoz (2nd ed. Indianapolis: Liberty Fund, 1998). Vol. 1. Chapter: 2: Joseph Sewall, NINEVEH'S REPENTANCE AND DELIVERANCE)

OLD TESTAMENT TEACHING ON THE SABBATH

Numbers 15:32-36 (NIV) [32] While the Israelites were in the desert, a man was found gathering wood on the Sabbath day. [33] Those who found him gathering wood brought him to Moses and Aaron and the whole assembly, [34] and they kept him in custody, because it was not clear what should be done to him. [35] Then the LORD said to Moses, "The man must die. The whole assembly must stone him outside the camp." [36] So the assembly took him outside the camp and stoned him to death, as the LORD commanded Moses.

It is very clear that the Lord was serious about obeying the Sabbath in the Old Testament. Is He as serious about our obedience in the New Testament? What other sins brought the death penalty in the Old Testament? Adultery, not honoring your parents, intentional murder. Serious sins had serious consequences. Not keeping the Sabbath holy was one of those sins. The Apostles and founders of our nation felt that the Sunday Sabbath should be honored as well. We know this from their faithful example of following God's Word.

There is no verse in the New Testament that specifically says, "Honor the Sabbath." But there are enough hints in Scripture that reveal the authority to obey is still there. Here are some of the "hints" that I have found in the New Testament:

THE TEN COMMANDMENTS ARE REINSTATED IN THE NEW TESTAMENT

Our generation is removing the Ten Commandments from public buildings. Some are even seeking to remove God from our nation altogether. The church and Christian families have already removed some of the commands from their own hearts. Why would the founders of our nation be so impressed to put the Ten Commandments on our buildings and in our courthouses? Did they only believe in nine of the ten or did they believe that all ten were equally important? They believed in all ten. They believed in obeying them as the commands state. They did so because the Ten Commandments are reinstated in the New Testament.

Look at what Jesus said to the man about how to gain eternal life. *Matthew 19:16-19 (NIV) ¹⁶ Now a man came up to Jesus and asked, "Teacher, what good thing must I do to get eternal life?" ¹⁷ "Why do you ask me about what is good?" Jesus replied. "There is only One who is good. If you want to enter life, obey the commandments."*

Jesus said, "If we want to enter life we must obey the commandments." Jesus goes on to tell us that we are to obey the Ten Commandments. *¹⁸ "Which ones?" the man inquired. Jesus replied, "'Do not murder, do not commit adultery, do not steal, do not give false testimony, ¹⁹ honor your father and mother,' and* *'love your neighbor as yourself.'"* Jesus reinstates the importance of obeying the Ten Commandments. Every single command He listed is one of the Ten Commandments. Some might argue and say, *"But He didn't specifically list the Sabbath command."* This is a true statement, but Jesus also didn't list idolatry, so are we free to commit idolatry in the New Testament? The fact is he listed only commandments that are in the Ten; reinstating their importance in the New Testament. Just because he did not list all ten definitely does not negate the importance of each one.

The book of James also reinstates the Ten Commandments in the New Testament. **James 2:10-11 (NIV) ¹⁰ For whoever keeps the <u>whole law</u> and yet stumbles at just one point is guilty of breaking all of it.** *¹¹ For he who said,* **"<u>Do not commit adultery</u>,"** *also said,* **"<u>Do not murder</u>."** *If you do not commit adultery but do commit murder, you have become a lawbreaker.*

The law that we are to obey in the New Testament is the Ten Commandments with the teachings of Christ. Our ability to obey the commands reveals that we have been born again. James says, *"If we stumble at just one point in the whole law we are guilty of breaking them all."* The law he is referring to is the Ten Commandments. We must obey the "whole" Ten Commandments just as the generations before us. We know that James is not referring to the sacrificial law or as some call it, the ceremonial law.

Christ fulfilled that with his death on the cross. Jesus was very clear with Peter that civil law, including dietary laws, were fulfilled as well.

The passage in James specifically mentions murder and adultery, but it also includes the whole law in verse 10. This means that we could interject any commandment into the teaching. Would idolatry work in the argument? Yes. Would stealing work in the argument? Yes. Would the Sabbath work in the argument? Yes. That is the point of the teaching. The whole law is important and none of the commands are to be forgotten or changed from their moral intentions.

Paul reinstates the Ten Commandments in *Romans 13:8-10 (NIV)* *⁸ Let no debt remain outstanding, except the continuing debt to love one another, for he who loves his fellowman has fulfilled the law. ⁹ The commandments, "Do not commit adultery," "Do not murder," "Do not steal," "Do not covet," **and whatever other commandment there may be**, are summed up in this one rule: "Love your neighbor as yourself." ¹⁰ Love does no harm to its neighbor. Therefore love is the fulfillment of the law.*

We are told by Jesus that the whole law can be summed up in these two commands: Love God and love your neighbor. The first four commands of the Ten Commandments are how we love God and the last six commandments are how we love our neighbor. None of the commandments are to be

70

excluded or changed. Love is the fulfillment of the law. The Ten Commandments help us apply the principles of love.

In this passage, Paul lists specific commands in the Ten Commandments and then says, **"and whatever other commandment there may be."** He was not excluding honoring your parents, honoring the Sabbath, or misusing God's name. **He said that whatever other commandment there may be we are to obey it to show that we love God and our neighbor as the law intends.**

Jesus, Paul, and James reinstate the importance of obeying the Ten Commandments in the New Testament. Look at what Jesus said in *Matthew 5:17-20 (NIV)* [17] *"Do not think that I have come to abolish the Law or the Prophets; I have not come to abolish them but to fulfill them.* [18] ***I tell you the truth, until heaven and earth disappear, not the smallest letter, not the least stroke of a pen, will by any means disappear from the Law until everything is accomplished.*** [19] *Anyone who breaks one of the least of these commandments and teaches others to do the same will be called least in the kingdom of heaven, but whoever practices and teaches these commands will be called great in the kingdom of heaven.* [20] *For I tell you that unless your righteousness surpasses that of the Pharisees and the teachers of the law, you will certainly not enter the kingdom of heaven.*

We are to practice and teach the Ten Commandments to others. Jesus begins to expound upon the Ten in the Sermon on the Mount. He brings up several of the Laws and then teaches us the heart of the matter and elevates their meaning. The verses that immediately follow this passage are Jesus expounding on some of the Ten Commandments.

Paul lists a law that we are to obey in *Romans 3:28-31* (NIV) [28] **For we maintain that a man is justified by faith apart from observing the law.** [29] Is God the God of Jews only? Is he not the God of Gentiles too? Yes, of Gentiles too, [30] since there is only one God, who will justify the circumcised by faith and the uncircumcised through that same faith. [31] Do we, then, nullify the law by this faith? Not at all! **Rather, we uphold the law.** What law are we to be upholding? The sacrificial? No. Jesus's sacrifice was once and for all and no more sacrifices are needed. The Civil laws? No. The Lord was very clear that the dietary laws were done away with and that we can eat meat. What law, then are we to be upholding? The moral law as has been revealed is reinstated in the New Testament. The moral law is the Ten Commandments.

JESUS HONORED THE SABBATH

The Scriptures clearly point out that Jesus obeyed the Sabbath command when it says in *Luke 4:16* (NIV) 16 He went to Nazareth, where he had been brought up, and on the **Sabbath day** he went into the synagogue, **as**

was his custom. What was the custom of Jesus? His custom was to be in the synagogue every Sabbath to worship with fellow believers. He remembered the Sabbath day and kept it holy.

The example of Christ is our greatest evidence of what we need to be doing in *1 John 2:6 (NIV)* *⁶ Whoever claims to live in him must walk as Jesus did.* Where would Jesus be on the Sabbath? What would he be doing on the Sabbath? What did He do and not do on the Sabbath?

Some misinterpret the teachings and actions of Jesus and they claim that He revealed to us that the Sabbath is no longer to be obeyed. This is heresy and completely untrue. The sacrifice of Christ had to be a sinless sacrifice to break the bondage of sin. If Christ broke any command prior to His sacrifice He would not have been a sinless sacrifice. Hebrews 4:15 tells us that Jesus was without sin. Therefore Jesus honored the Sabbath.

The issues that Jesus dealt with were the legalistic views of the Pharisees. Rules that were written by the Pharisees as to how the term "work" would be interpreted placed a heavy burden upon the people. Jesus consequently talked a lot about the intent of the Sabbath in the New Testament.
In John, Jesus claimed to be "working on the Sabbath." Some interpret this as a passage that

excludes the Sabbath command in the New Testament. In John, Chapter 5, Jesus healed a paralyzed man on the Sabbath and the Pharisees accused him again. *John 5:16-17 (NIV) [16] So, because Jesus was doing these things on the Sabbath, the Jews persecuted him. [17] Jesus said to them,* **"My Father is always at his work to this very day, and I, too, am working."**

Is Jesus saying that working on the Sabbath is permitted? No. He is not saying it is okay to work on the Sabbath; He is claiming to be equal with God. The verse says, *"My Father is always at his work to this very day, and I, too, am working."* The Jewish belief is that God does not rest on the Sabbath anymore because He is always working. God rested at creation to establish the sacred day and to reveal to His creations His intent for the day. The belief that God no longer rests is seen in the fact that the sun still rises on the Sabbath, babies are still born on the Sabbath, and the rain still comes on the Sabbath. These actions have been interpreted as God always working since God does not need to rest.

The Pharisees knew that Jesus was claiming deity. *John 5:18 (NIV) [18] For this reason the Jews tried all the harder to kill him; not only was he breaking the Sabbath, but he was even calling God his own Father, making himself equal with God.*

The Pharisees considered Jesus healing people as working on the Sabbath. Jesus clarified that for us in

Matthew 12:12 (NIV) ¹² How much more valuable is a man than a sheep! Therefore it is lawful to do good on the Sabbath."

Jesus was a sinless sacrifice. Jesus was "not working" on the Sabbath. He was God.

JESUS' FOLLOWERS HONORED THE SABBATH

This is powerful evidence that Jesus intends for us to obey the command today. If Jesus meant to reveal to us that we no longer needed to rest on the Sabbath, then His followers would have followed this teaching. The evidence that they did not is not only historical but it is also Biblical. The Bible states how His followers obeyed the Sabbath.

The Bible reveals how people rested on the Sabbath while Jesus was with them. But Scriptures also reveal that people followed this command after His death. *So for three years they walked with Christ and heard His teachings and followed His lead.* If Jesus was teaching His followers that they no longer needed to rest on the Sabbath, why does the Bible specifically point out that they rested in obedience to the command?

After Jesus was crucified, Mary Magdalene, Mary the mother of James, and Salome went to purchase spices to anoint the body of Jesus. Scriptures clearly state that they waited until the Sabbath was over to buy them. Why? Why would they wait? Why did they not just go and purchase the spices? They knew that would cause another to work on the Sabbath, so they rested in obedience to what Christ had taught them. *Mark 16:1 (NIV)* *¹ **When the Sabbath was over**, Mary Magdalene, Mary the mother of James, and Salome bought spices so that they might go to anoint Jesus' body.*

Luke's gospel points out the fact that they rested on the Sabbath, as well. Not only did the women wait to purchase the spices until after the Sabbath, but they waited to prepare the spices and perfumes until the Sabbath was over. *Luke 23:56 (NIV)* *⁵⁶ Then they went home and prepared spices and perfumes.* **But they rested on the Sabbath in obedience to the commandment.**

These passages are evidence that Christ still desires for us to honor the Sabbath. The followers of Jesus obeyed the fourth commandment by resting on the Sabbath. We know this from both history and Scripture. In Biblical times, dead bodies decayed so quickly that people made spices and perfumes to cover the odor. The women could have said, *"This is an emergency we need to prepare Jesus' body."* Instead they obeyed what Jesus had taught them and they rested on the Sabbath in obedience to the commandment. Why does Scripture point this out in the New Testament? To reinstate the importance of this commandment for us today!

Some may argue that the disciples did not know they were free from the Sabbath law since these two passages occurred before the resurrection. However, other passages in Acts reveal to us how the disciples continued to honor the Sabbath. Jesus spent over forty days with the Apostles and taught them after His resurrection. *Acts 1:3 (NIV) ³ After his suffering, he showed himself to these men and gave many convincing proofs that he was alive. He appeared to them over a period of forty days and spoke about the kingdom of God.* This would have been a great opportunity for Christ to reveal to His disciples that they no longer needed to heed the commands of the Sabbath and its stipulations.

Here is the command as stated in *Exodus 20:8-11 (NIV) ⁸ "Remember the Sabbath day by keeping it holy. ⁹ Six days you shall labor and do all your work, ¹⁰ but the seventh day is a Sabbath to the LORD your God. On it you shall not do any work, neither you, nor your son or daughter, nor your manservant or maidservant, nor your animals, nor the alien within your gates. ¹¹ For in six days the LORD made the heavens and the earth, the sea, and all that is in them, but he rested on the seventh day. Therefore the LORD blessed the Sabbath day and made it holy.*

We have already seen how the followers of Jesus would not work or purchase things on Sunday. In this passage, we get a glimpse of how serious it was to keep from doing anything too strenuous on the Lord's Day. Many disciples called Sunday the Lord's Day to distinguish it from the Jewish Sabbath. They followed the same stipulations of the command for Sunday.

The Day of Pentecost happened on a Sunday. Pentecost is also called the feast of weeks; feast of harvest; the day of first fruits to be celebrated 50 days after the Passover. *Leviticus 23:15-16 (NIV)* *15 "**From the day after the Sabbath**, the day you brought the sheaf of the wave offering, count off seven full weeks. 16 Count off **fifty days** up to **the day after the seventh Sabbath**, and then present an offering of new grain to the LORD.*

The day after the Sabbath would be Sunday, because the Jewish Sabbath is Saturday. The Jews were to count fifty days after Passover to know what day to celebrate Pentecost. It would then fall after the Saturday Sabbath. In the Old Testament, the first Passover occurred when the nation of Israel was delivered out of the hand of slavery from Pharaoh. Fifty days after the first Passover, God gave Moses the law and established Israel as a nation. Now fifty days after Christ's death, on Passover, He establishes the church.

The Bible reveals to us that the disciples moved the Sabbath from Saturday to Sunday and began meeting together for worship. *Acts 2:1 (NIV)*

¹ When the day of Pentecost came, they were all together in one place. Here we see the disciples were worshiping together on Sunday. The Holy Spirit falls on them and establishes the church.

The Bible says in *Acts 1:12-13 (NIV) ¹² Then they returned to Jerusalem from the hill called the Mount of Olives, a **Sabbath day's walk from the city**. ¹³ When they arrived, they went upstairs to the room where they were staying. Those present were…*

Scripture reveals that on this Sunday they went to the room to meet together; only walking a Sabbath day's walk. A Sabbath day's walk was about ¾ of a mile. Anything beyond that was considered strenuous and working on the Sabbath. We know that the day of Pentecost fell on Sunday, the day after the Saturday Jewish Sabbath. Why would the Scriptures reveal to us that they only walked a Sabbath day's walk? It was to show that the day changed but the stipulations to the command remained.

BELIEVERS ENTER THE SABBATH REST

Jesus came not to exclude the fourth commandment, but to reveal to us how it should be obeyed. The Sabbath was made for man. God's intentions, even at creation, are for us to be blessed by our obedience on the Sabbath. There is a passage in Hebrews that addresses the topic of Sabbath rest for the people of

God. It has a lot to do with our humility and our willingness to enter that rest.

It says in *Hebrews 3:14-19 (NIV)* *[14] We have come to share in Christ if we hold firmly till the end the confidence we had at first. [15] As has just been said: "Today, if you hear his voice, do not harden your hearts as you did in the rebellion." [16] Who were they who heard and rebelled? Were they not all those Moses led out of Egypt? [17] And with whom was he angry for forty years? Was it not with those who sinned, whose bodies fell in the desert? [18] And to whom did God swear that they would never enter his rest if not to those who disobeyed? [19] So we see that they were not able to enter, because of their unbelief.*

In verse 18, the word disobeyed can also be translated disbelieved. The writer is warning believers to stand firm until the end in their obedience to Christ. He uses an illustration from the Old Testament to point out that their unbelief produced disobedience and they were not able to enter into the rest.

Many of these people had rested on the Sabbath as the law requires, so the rest that Hebrews is speaking of is a heavenly rest. Believers will one day enter into a heavenly rest, or a completed rest, as God rested when He completed His creation.
The key to entering this heavenly rest is obedience verses disobedience. Unbelief produces disobedience and belief produces obedience.

Hebrews 4:1-5 (NIV) [1] Therefore, since the promise of entering his rest still stands, let us be careful that none of you be found to have fallen short of it. [2] For we also have had the gospel preached to us, just as they did; but the message they heard was of no value to them, because those who heard did not combine it with faith. [3] Now we who have believed enter that rest, just as God has said, "So I declared on oath in my anger, 'They shall never enter my rest.'" And yet his work has been finished since the creation of the world. [4] For somewhere he has spoken about the seventh day in these words: "And on the seventh day God rested from all his work." [5] And again in the passage above he says, "They shall never enter my rest."

Who will never enter into God's heavenly rest? Those who do not combine the message with faith and walk in obedience to God's commands. The passage continues in *Hebrews 4:6-8 (NIV) [6] It still remains that some will enter that rest, and those who formerly had the gospel preached to them **did not go in, because of their disobedience.** [7] Therefore God again set a certain day, calling it Today, when a long time later he spoke through David, as was said before: "Today, if you hear his voice, do not harden your hearts." [8] For if Joshua had given them rest, God would not have spoken later about another day.*

What is this believers' rest and how do we enter it? *Hebrews 4:9-11 (NIV) [9] **There remains, then, a Sabbath-rest for the people of God;** [10] for anyone who enters God's rest also rests from his own work, just*

81

as God did from his. **¹¹ Let us, therefore, make every effort to enter that rest, so that no one will fall by following their example of disobedience.**
We are told that we need to be making every effort to enter into this Sabbath rest, but what is the key? The key is that as God rested from His work we must also rest from our own work. As it says, *"for anyone who enters God's rest also rests from his own work, just as God did from his."*

Jesus said it this way in *Matthew 11:28-30 (NIV)* ²⁸ *"Come to me, all you who are weary and burdened, and I will give you rest.* ²⁹ *Take my yoke upon you and learn from me, for I am gentle and humble in heart, and you will find rest for your souls.* ³⁰ *For my yoke is easy and my burden is light."*

The yoke of God is His authority in our lives. When an oxen has a yoke placed on his neck, it is a heavy wooden harness with ropes tied to it. It allows the master to steer the animal where he wants him to go. This is where the Old Testament Sabbath and humility intersect to produce obedience in us. Humility is to be totally dependent upon God and His ability to sustain, provide, protect, and bless. God is the one who fills us with His Holy Spirit and enables us to walk in obedience. Without taking His yoke upon us, and receiving the Holy Spirit, we would not obey God's commands. **The Sabbath is a sacred day. When we humble ourselves and treat the day as God designed, we are blessed by Him and enabled to obey His commands.**

Exodus 31:13 (NIV) [13] Say to the Israelites, You must observe my Sabbaths. This will be a sign between me and you for the generations to come, so you may know that I am the LORD, **who makes you holy .** God's Word promises us blessings as we remember the day and keep it holy. God promises to make us holy. We have been freed from fulfilling other Old Testament ceremonial and civil law, but we have not been freed from the Ten Commandment law to "keep the Sabbath holy."

When we work on the Sabbath, or cause others to work on the Sabbath, we are revealing our arrogance and trust in ourselves. When we treat the day as God intended, we show the world who we are trusting and that we acknowledge Him for blessing us. God is the one who has blessed America and He is the one who protects America. If we fail to obey God, we will lose His protection and blessings. We will have the curses the covenant promises to all who disobey God's commands. Curses like debt, lack of protection, and losing our freedoms.

To do as we please on the Sabbath is evidence of our unbelief in who God is and His provision for our lives and our nation. We have become proud. We feel like we do not need to follow all ten of His commandments anymore. The Apostles, early church, great preachers, and the founders of America all understood the importance of entering into the rest of obedience.

The Apostles believed in obeying all Ten of the Commandments. The founders of our nation believed in obeying all Ten. Their generations saw God do amazing things and experienced His blessings. Our generation disagrees with obeying the Sabbath and we are experiencing God's curses. Which side should we choose? Those who believed we should obey all Ten or our current generation? I'm choosing to side with the Apostles and founders of America.
When the church rests on the Sabbath it is a sign to the world. It is also a time for God to make us holy and strengthen us for the week ahead.

Exodus 31:14-17 (NIV) [14] "'Observe the Sabbath, because it is holy to you. Anyone who desecrates it must be put to death; whoever does any work on that day must be cut off from his people. [15] For six days, work is to be done, but the seventh day is a Sabbath of rest, holy to the LORD. Whoever does any work on the Sabbath day must be put to death. [16] The Israelites are to observe the Sabbath, celebrating it for the generations to come as a lasting covenant. [17] **It will be a sign between me and the Israelites <u>forever</u>,** *for in six days the LORD made the heavens and the earth, and on the seventh day he abstained from work and rested.'"*

This is to be a sign forever! One of the greatest witnesses we can have as the church is how we keep the day holy. What would businesses do if Christians stopped eating out on Sunday? Many of them would most likely close from the lack of Sunday business. What would sporting events do if all of those who claim to be Christians stopped supporting them on Sunday? They would move to Saturday or another day of the week. We could be a powerful witness to the world by the way we treat the Sabbath. We are to work six days and then rest on the Sabbath in obedience to God's command. He is our God. He is the one who sustains us, provides for us, and protects us. He has promised to bless us for our careful obedience to His commands.

Look at this passage in *Isaiah 58:12-14 (NIV)* *[12] Your people will rebuild the ancient ruins and will raise up the age-old foundations; you will be called Repairer of Broken Walls, Restorer of Streets with Dwellings. [13] "If you keep your feet from breaking the Sabbath and from doing as you please on my holy day, if you call the Sabbath a delight and the LORD's holy day honorable, and if you honor it by not going your own way and not doing as you please or speaking idle words, [14] then you will find your joy in the LORD, and I will cause you to ride on the heights of the land and to feast on the inheritance of your father Jacob." The mouth of the LORD has spoken.* **It says that the nation will be called repairer and restorer if we obey the Sabbath.** The command of the Sabbath is to rest. How will the nation be able to repair and restore when it is resting on the Sabbath? God will do it through us if we will rest from our work and allow Christ to live through us. God is the one who sanctifies and restores. He does it for those who will submit to His authority and call Jesus Lord.

Can we change any of the Commandments? Can we change what adultery is? Can we change what coveting is? Can we change what false testimony is? Can we change the stipulations in the command to keep the Sabbath holy? No we cannot! We are not to take away or add to God's commands.

Let's follow the example of the Apostles, founders, and other great generations who experienced the blessings of God. Let's again honor the Sabbath! Something very powerful happens to believers who delight in the Sabbath and do not go their own way. God makes us Holy as we rest in His presence and worship Him.

WORKSHEET FOR CHURCH GOVERNMENT
LIFE TRUTH # 3
THE CHURCH HONORS THE SABBATH

Question: How should the church view the Sabbath?

Answer: The church should rest on the Sabbath in obedience to the command.

Luke 23:56 (NIV) {superscript 56} Then they went home and prepared spices and perfumes. But they rested on the Sabbath in obedience to the commandment. Underline or highlight the verse. Write these corresponding verse references next to Luke 23:56 – Exodus 31:12-17; Isaiah 58:13

> Write out the Life Truth, question, and answer on one side of an index card and the verse on the other side. Keep it in your Bible for the week. Work on it every day individually and as a family. Have it memorized by next week.

Read Exodus 20:8-11. The passage says in Luke 23:56 that they rested in obedience to the command. What does "rested" mean?

Read Numbers 15:32-36. What was the punishment for those who would not obey the Sabbath?

Who said the man must die?

Read Isaiah 58:12-14. What does the nation of Israel need to do to be called, "Repairer of Broken Walls, Restorer of Streets with Dwelling?

Read Romans 2:17-24. Verse 24 says that, "God's name is blasphemed among the Gentiles." The reason is that they are not obeying the Ten Commandments. What three of the Ten Commandments are listed in this passage?

Read Matthew 5:17-20. What law do you think Christ is referring to?
What law does Jesus refer to in Matthew 5:21?

According to Matthew 5:18. Would it be OK to work or to cause someone to work on the Sabbath?

According to Matthew 5:19. If we are "breaking the Sabbath" by working or causing others to work what will we be called in the Kingdom of Heaven?

Read Exodus 31:13. What is a sign between the nation and God?
Who makes the nation holy?

Read Exodus 31:14-17. What is a lasting covenant and sign between God forever?

The Apostles moved the Sabbath from Saturday to Sunday in the New Testament. Sunday is the first day of the week. Read Acts 20:7; 1 Corinthians 16:2. Why do you think God moved the Sabbath?

Based on this LIFE TRUTH what can you do individually and as a family to be more devoted to the Sabbath? How can you help others see the importance of obeying the Sabbath Command?

CHURCH-GOVERNMENT LIFE TRUTH # 4
THE CHURCH HONORS GOD WITH THEIR TITHES AND OFFERINGS

Most people don't like to talk about money; especially when it affects their own wallets. Many even have an attitude that no one has the right to tell them what to do with their money. In general, people just want to spend their money exactly how they choose. People are interested in a good financial investment, however. What if you heard there was a sure way to increase your wealth? Would you be interested in hearing more?

Tithing is the best financial decision anyone can make. God promises to bless those who bring in their tithes and offerings. A tithe is a tenth of what you have. If you have a hundred dollars, then ten dollars would be a tithe. When you tithe, you bring a tenth of what the Lord has blessed you with and give it back to Him. We are to tithe out of our thankfulness to God; for He is good. In the Bible, people would tithe not only monetary amounts but also a tenth of their cattle, grain, and other crops. If God blessed a family with 50 heads of cattle, they would tithe 5 back to Him. If He blessed them with a good harvest, they would return ten percent of it as a tithe.

Tithing has been around since the beginning of creation. Abraham, Jacob, and many others tithed.

During the time of Moses, God gave the people specific instructions about tithing. The people understood that offerings were different than tithes because offerings were not set amounts. A tithe is ten percent but an offering is any percentage. Offerings are to be given in addition to tithes. An offering is an opportunity to thank God by helping to meet the needs of His people.

Jacob had an encounter with God and vowed to tithe all that the Lord had blessed him with. *Genesis 28:10-22 (NIV) [10] Jacob left Beersheba and set out for Haran. [11] When he reached a certain place, he stopped for the night because the sun had set. Taking one of the stones there, he put it under his head and lay down to sleep. [12] He had a dream in which he saw a stairway resting on the earth, with its top reaching to heaven, and the angels of God were ascending and descending on it. [13] There above it stood the LORD, and he said: "I am the LORD, the God of your father Abraham and the God of Isaac. I will give you and your descendants the land on which you are lying. [14] Your descendants will be like the dust of the earth, and you will spread out to the west and to the east, to the north and to the south. All peoples on earth will be blessed through you and your offspring. [15] I am with you and will watch over you wherever you go, and I will bring you back to this land. I will not leave you until I have done what I have promised you." [16] When Jacob awoke from his sleep, he thought, "Surely the LORD is in this place, and I was not aware of it." [17] He was afraid and said, "How awesome is this place! This is none other than the house of God; this is the gate of heaven." [18] Early the* *next morning Jacob took the stone he had placed under his head and set it up as a pillar and poured oil on top of it. [19] He called that place Bethel, though the city used to be called Luz. [20] Then Jacob made a vow, saying, "If God will be with me and will watch over me on this journey I am taking and will give me food to eat and clothes to wear [21] so that I return safely to my father's house, then the LORD will be my God [22] and this stone that I have set up as a pillar will be God's house, **and of all that you give me I will give you a tenth.**"*

Jacob came to realize that God was his provider, protector, and sustainer. His experience with God caused him to respond in thankfulness and honor. He made a vow to give a tenth of all that God would bless him with. God is longing for us to realize that He is our provider. He wants us to worship him with our tithes and offerings. When we give back to God it shows our dependence upon Him, our thankfulness to Him, and our trust in Him. God does not **need** what we have because He already owns it all. We **need** to give back to God to reveal what's really in our hearts. Tithing shows that we trust God for our daily provisions and protection.

One of God's greatest characteristics is that He is gracious. He is a giver. He desires to bless others with what He has. He has done this in so many ways, but the greatest way was when He gave His son to die on the cross for us.

God desires that we mature in character and become like Him. We are to grow in the grace of giving. *2 Corinthians 8:7 (NIV) [7] But just as you excel in everything—in faith, in speech, in knowledge, in complete earnestness and in your love for us—see that you also excel in this grace of giving.*

To grow in the grace of giving, we must first understand that we are stewards and not owners of what we have. God owns everything. He loans us the money, possessions, bodies, and whatever else we have to use for His glory. We are not the owners. We are just the managers of His property. With this new perspective, we can release our selfish, tightfisted mindsets regarding the blessings the Lord has given us.

The church of Acts had a great mindset about being God's stewards. We can learn two very important principles from them.

PRINCIPLES OF STEWARDSHIP

1. We do not own our possessions

Acts 4:32-35 (NIV) [32] All the believers were one in heart and mind. No one claimed that any of his possessions was his own, but they shared everything they had. No one in the church claimed that any of their possessions were their own. Do you have a special something that you would never want anyone else to have or use? The early church didn't have such a mindset. They shared everything they had.

Many times we use the term *steward* to justify our selfishness. We think that since God gave us this "possession" we must protect it from those who may not take care of it as well as we do. We justify not sharing it with others to satisfy our own selfishness. Look at what Jesus said in the Sermon on the Mount in *Matthew 5:38-42 (NIV)* *[38] "You have heard that it was said, 'Eye for eye, and tooth for tooth.' [39] But I tell you, Do not resist **an evil person**. If someone strikes you on the right cheek, turn to him the other also. [40] And if someone wants to sue you and take your tunic, let him have your cloak as well. [41] If someone forces you to go one mile, go with him two miles. [42] **Give to the one who asks you, and do not turn away from the one who wants to borrow from you.***

This passage says we are not to resist an evil person. Are we ready to give to anyone who asks? Are we willing to loan to those who want to borrow from us? Would we loan our best or give people our leftovers?

Our mindset needs to change. We need to become more like God in the area of stewardship. We are to bless others.

The following passage in Acts shows a deep love for one another and a lack of love for the things of this world. It helps us to look at our possessions with a more heavenly perspective. *Acts 4:32-35 (NIV)* *³² All the believers were one in heart and mind. No one claimed that any of his possessions was his own, but they shared everything they had. ³³ With great power the apostles continued to testify to the resurrection of the Lord Jesus, and much grace was upon them all. ³⁴ There were no needy persons among them. For from time to time those who owned lands or houses sold them, brought the money from the sales ³⁵ and put it at the apostles' feet, and it was distributed to anyone as he had need.*

The early believers would sell their possessions and give their money to the church so it could be distributed to anyone who had a need. This is a great description of an offering. It is not a tithe or something that God expects to be brought in. Offerings are to be given for the benefit of others.

In our self-centered society, we are consumed with what we want, what we have, and what we think we need. This was definitely not the mindset of the early church. They were so aware of the needs of others that there were no needy persons among them.

This should be the mindset of every local church. Leaders should know their members well enough to address their needs when times get tough. They are not to enable people to live in sin or be unproductive in society, however. But as issues happen in this world, the church is to help each other out.

The passage says that much grace was upon them all. It does not say that much grace was upon the ones who sold land or houses; much grace was upon them all. They were one in heart and mind. God was blessing them greatly as they walked in obedience and love.

There are three specific reasons for the tithe in the Old Testament.

1. For Fellowship

The nation of Israel would get together every year and celebrate together with a feast. The feast was from the tithes that people brought in. God loves it when we fellowship together and celebrate His goodness to us. *Deuteronomy 14:22-29 (NIV) ²² Be sure to set aside a tenth of all that your fields produce each year. ²³ Eat the tithe of your grain, new wine and oil, and the firstborn of your herds and flocks in the presence of the LORD your God at the place he will choose as a dwelling for his Name, so that you may learn to revere the LORD your God always. ²⁴ But if that place is too distant and you have been blessed by the LORD your God and cannot carry your tithe (because the place where the LORD will choose to put his Name is so far away), ²⁵ then exchange your tithe for silver, and take the silver with you and go to the place the LORD your God will choose. ²⁶ Use the silver to buy whatever you like: cattle, sheep, wine or other fermented drink, or anything you wish. Then you and your household shall eat there in the presence of the LORD your God and rejoice.*

Notice that if the place was too far to travel, the family was to still spend time together rejoicing in God's goodness. It is still good for us to take breaks and fellowship in the Lord together.

Churches, in our generation, need to have fellowships together. Fellowships will help us to get to know one another so we can better minister to the needs of people around us. If we never fellowship together how will we get to know one another? The Bible teaches that we are to use some of the tithe money that is brought into the storehouse for fellowships

2. To Provide for the Levites

The Levites took care of the temple. They performed the sacrifices and taught the people. With all of their responsibilities, they were unable to work their own land. The tithe was to provide for their needs. *Numbers 18:20-21 (NIV) [20] The LORD said to Aaron, "You will have no inheritance in their land, nor will you have any share among them; I am your share and your inheritance among the Israelites. [21] "I give to the Levites all the tithes in Israel as their inheritance in return for the work they do while serving at the Tent of Meeting.*

The Levites lived off of the tithes that came in. In the New Testament, Paul reinstates the command to care for ministers through the tithes. *I Corinthians 9:13-14 (NIV) [13] Don't you know that those who work in the temple get their food from the temple, and those who serve at the altar share in what is offered on the altar? ¹⁴ In the same way, the Lord has commanded that those who preach the gospel should receive their living from the gospel.*

3. To Provide for the Needy

The tithes were to be used to provide for those in need in their fellowship and for the people around them. *Deuteronomy 14:28-29 (NIV) ²⁸ At the end of every three years, bring all the tithes of that year's produce and store it in your towns, ²⁹ so that the Levites (who have no allotment or inheritance of their own) and the aliens, the fatherless and the widows who live in your towns may come and eat and be satisfied, and so that the LORD your God may bless you in all the work of your hands.*

The word *aliens* refers to those who were not part of the nation of Israel. Even though they were not a part of the nation, God wanted the nation to help them.

Here are three Biblical principles for the tithes that we can apply to our lives today:
1. We can use the tithes for fellowships and celebrations.
2. We can use the tithes to care for our buildings and for those who serve in our church.
3. We can use the tithes to provide for those in need.

Some may argue that the tithe is Old Testament law and not reinstated in the New Testament. The fact is that Jesus himself reinstated the tithe in the New Testament when He was giving His woes to the Pharisees. *Luke 11:42 (NIV) [42] "Woe to you Pharisees, because you give God a tenth of your mint, rue and all other kinds of garden herbs, but you neglect justice and the love of God. You should have practiced the latter without leaving the former undone.*

Jesus condemned the Pharisees for not being loving and not seeking true justice for others. He did not condemn their tithing, however. In fact, He stated that they needed to be doing both. The Gospel of Matthew also presents this passage and reinstates tithing in the New Testament. Jesus is telling us not only to tithe, even to our spice rack, but also to love our neighbor as ourselves.

It is a dangerous time for a society when the people of God begin to focus more on themselves and their property than on ministering to others and giving to those in need. The church today is to be like the church of Acts. We should not consider our possessions as our own. Instead, we should see them as resources to be used for God's glory. Everything that we own is God's. We are to share it with those who have a need.

Idolatry is when we love something more than God. If you own something that you would not want to share, lend, or give to another, then that "thing" owns you. Our hearts must be cautious of idolatry. We are commanded to have no idols before the Lord. God has called the church to bring in tithes and offerings so that others can be blessed. Tithes and offerings are a part of God's design to reveal His love to a lost and dying world.

If every American who claimed to be a Christian actually brought in their tithes and offerings, we could stop the hunger in this world. We could afford to provide Bibles for everyone. We could even begin to pay off our national debt. But selfishness and greed are destroying our nation.

Some may say, *"If I had more I would give more."* This is just another excuse to justify why they do not give. Jesus praised the widow in Mark, Chapter 12, because she gave all that she had. In 2 Corinthians, Chapter 8, we learn that the Macedonian churches gave beyond their means. They sacrificed so that others could be blessed.

Everyday God reveals that HE LOVE US! He gives us new mercies every morning. He does not treat us as our sins deserve.

Lamentations 3:22-23 (NIV) [22] *Because of the LORD's great love we are not consumed, for his compassions never fail.* [23] *They are new every morning; great is your faithfulness.*

Psalm 103:10-11 (NIV) ⁰ he does not treat us as our sins deserve or repay us according to our iniquities. ¹¹ For as high as the heavens are above the earth, so great is his love for those who fear him;

Romans tells us that God pours His love into our hearts. With that kind of love, how can we treat others with condemnation and judgment? The Pharisees were accused of being harsh, without love and mercy. Could the same be said of this generation? Are we so consumed with what we have that we are unwilling to share our possessions with the people who really need them?

Offerings are to be heartfelt and given with a cheerful attitude. Christians should have such a love for others that as needs arise they want to help. Some may even sacrifice by giving more than they have so that others can be blessed. Is this not the example that Jesus left for us? But how can we bring in the offerings when we're not bringing in the tithes? We are commanded to bring in the tithes and offerings. Scholars have tried to justify the idea that we do not have to do such things today, but Paul clearly says in

2 Corinthians 8:12-15 (NIV) ¹² For if the willingness is there, the gift is acceptable according to what one has, not according to what he does not have. ¹³ Our desire is not that others might be relieved while you are hard pressed, but that there might be equality. ¹⁴ At the present time your plenty will supply what they need, so that in turn their plenty will supply what you need. Then there will be equality, ⁱ⁵ as it is written: "He who gathered much did not have too much, and he who gathered little did not have too little."

Paul told the church in his first letter how to raise money for an offering. *I Corinthians 16:1-3 (NIV)*
¹ Now about the collection for God's people: Do what I told the Galatian churches to do. ² On the first day of every week, each one of you should set aside a sum of money in keeping with his income, saving it up, so that when I come no collections will have to be made. ³ Then, when I arrive, I will give letters of introduction to the men you approve and send them with your gift to Jerusalem.

Not only did he tell the church of Corinth about ways for raising money but he told the Galatian churches as well. Notice the day of the week that the church met; the first day of the week. This is just another example in Scripture that shows us the Sabbath was moved from Saturday to Sunday.
The body of Christ accomplishes much when it works together. If one family gives $50 to meet a need, it's only a small amount of help; but if 20 families give $50 each to meet a need, the gift of $1000 becomes a big amount of help. Together we can do so much more.

This is God's design for the church. First, we make sure that there are no needy persons among us. Second, we begin to meet the needs in our community. Third, we listen to the prompting of the Holy Spirit to see if there are other needs that we should meet. This passage reminds us to make sure the believers are taken care of. *Galatians 6:10 (NIV) ¹⁰ Therefore, as we have opportunity, let us do good to all people, especially to those who belong to the family of believers.*

Has God blessed us with a generous crop so that we might be able to help another? Have we gathered much so that there might be equality? A willingness in the heart is what God is looking for. Paul says in *2 Corinthians 9:6-15 (NIV) ⁶ Remember this: Whoever sows sparingly will also reap sparingly, and whoever sows generously will also reap generously. ⁷ Each man should give what he has decided in his heart to give, not reluctantly or under compulsion, for God loves a cheerful giver. ⁸ And God is able to make all grace abound to you, so that in all things at all times, having all that you need, you will abound in every good work. ⁹ As it is written: "He has scattered abroad his gifts to the poor; his righteousness endures forever." ¹⁰ Now he who supplies seed to the sower and bread for food will also supply and increase your store of seed and will enlarge the harvest of your righteousness. ¹¹ You will be made rich in every way so that you can be generous on every occasion, and through us your generosity will result in thanksgiving to God. ¹² This service that you perform is not only supplying the needs of God's people but is also overflowing in many expressions of thanks to God. ¹³ Because of the service by which you have proved yourselves, men will praise God for the obedience that accompanies your confession of the gospel of Christ, and for your generosity in sharing with them and with everyone else. ¹⁴ And in their prayers for* *you their hearts will go out to you, because of the surpassing grace God has given you. ¹⁵ Thanks be to God for his indescribable gift!*

Some have interpreted this passage to say that tithing is no longer required in the New Testament. They use this passage and quote where it says that we can choose what we want to give. The passage is clearly talking about an offering and not the tithe. In fact, Paul calls it just that a few verses prior in *2 Corinthians 8:19 (NIV) ¹⁹ What is more, he was chosen by the churches to accompany us as we carry* **the offering**. There is a Biblical distinction between the two. The tithe is holy and it belongs to the Lord. Offerings are up to us to give as the Spirit prompts and leads.

Our cheerful giving blesses God. It brings praise to God. If we sow generously God will bless us. If we sow sparingly, we will reap sparingly. Are you going through a dry time spiritually? Have you missed or passed up an opportunity to give cheerfully to someone? Our righteousness is tied to our giving. The passage states that we will receive a harvest of righteousness if we are a generous cheerful giver. Offerings are opportunities to give what God confirms for us in our hearts. Offerings are given for God's glory. He determines the amount. We just need to be willing to listen to His voice and give the offering cheerfully.

It is important for parents to teach their children to tithe. As soon as they start getting birthday presents and earning money, children need to begin tithing. Little ones can also learn to be sensitive to the Holy Spirit when He prompts them to meet a need. Parents need to be ready to help when God uses a child's heart to do His work.

Jesus said in *Luke 12:33-34 (NIV)* *[33] Sell your possessions and give to the poor. Provide purses for yourselves that will not wear out, a treasure in heaven that will not be exhausted, where no thief comes near and no moth destroys. [34] For where your treasure is, there your heart will be also.*

There is a powerful passage in Malachi about tithes and offerings. *Malachi 3:6-18 (NIV) [6] "I the LORD do not change. So you, O descendants of Jacob, are not destroyed. [7] Ever since the time of your forefathers you have turned away from my decrees and have not kept them. Return to me, and I will return to you," says the LORD Almighty. "But you ask, 'How are we to return?' [8] "Will a man rob God? Yet you rob me. "But you ask, 'How do we rob you?' "In tithes and offerings.*

God spoke through his prophet that we rob Him when we do not bring in our tithes and offerings. Remember Jesus did not condemn the Pharisees for being careful with their tithing, even in the smallest blessings, but he condemned them for not having love and justice in combination with their passion to tithe. Tithes and offerings do not earn us salvation but they are evidence as to how much we love and honor God.

Christians should never take the money that is designated for the tithe and give it as an offering. Offerings are to be given over and above the tithe. If we use our tithe to help another, we have stolen money from God. God has asked us to give ten percent back to Him. The Bible is clear that the tithe is the Lord's. It is set apart as holy.

Look at what it says in Leviticus about people who keep their tithes. *Leviticus 27:30-33 (NIV) 30 "'A tithe of everything from the land, whether grain from the soil or fruit from the trees, belongs to the LORD; it is holy to the LORD. 31 If a man redeems any of his tithe, he must add a fifth of the value to it. 32 The entire tithe of the herd and flock—every tenth animal that passes under the shepherd's rod—will be holy to the LORD. 33 He must not pick out the good from the bad or make any substitution. If he does make a substitution, both the animal and its substitute become holy and cannot be redeemed.'"*
It says in *Proverbs 3:9-10 (NIV) 9 Honor the LORD with your wealth, with the first fruits of all your crops; 10 then your barns will be filled to overflowing, and your vats will brim over with new wine.* Many times people struggle financially because they refuse to bring in the first fruits of their tithes and offerings. Remember God was pleased with Abel's offering because he brought in the best; but with Cain's offering of leftovers God was not pleased.

There is a promise in tithing. If we obey God in this area, He will bless us. Our storehouses will be overflowing. The overflowing is not for our consumption, however. It is for us to take care of God's house and to minister to the poor and needy in the land.

Malachi, Chapter 3, goes on to say, *⁹ You are under a curse–the whole nation of you–because you are robbing me. ¹⁰ Bring the whole tithe into the storehouse, that there may be food in my house. Test me in this," says the LORD Almighty, "and see if I will not throw open the floodgates of heaven and pour out so much blessing that you will not have room enough for it. ¹¹ I will prevent pests from devouring your crops, and the vines in your fields will not cast their fruit," says the LORD Almighty.*

There is a curse for not bringing in the tithe and offerings. You may argue that you can't bring in the tithe because you don't make enough money. The truth is not that you can't afford to tithe. It's that you have chosen to live beyond your means with what the Lord has blessed you with. The real truth is that you can't afford **not** to tithe. Set aside your tithe first and then figure out what you can live on.

We need to repent and ask God to forgive us for not bringing in the whole tithe. It is time to start obeying this command. Should we wait until we get out of debt before we tithe? Should we wait until we lower our monthly bills? No. We need to begin tithing on the first fruits of every paycheck now. Ten percent of all income we receive belongs to the Lord. Our vow should be like Jacob's; a vow to tithe on everything that the Lord provides for us.

Many of our financial issues are a result of not bringing in the whole tithe to God. God promises to protect us from things that can destroy our wealth when we tithe. Tithing is a sign that we trust God. When we refuse to tithe and bring in our offerings, it reveals a selfishness and lack of love for others. God can be trusted. We need to bring in the tithes and offerings and watch God begin to overflow our church checking accounts. We are to show the world that God loves them. We are to meet needs and minister to the orphans, the widows, and the poor in our community. The more we have, the more we can do in our communities to show people that God loves them.

Malachi 3 tells us what will happen when we obey God in this area. [12] *"Then all the nations will call you blessed, for yours will be a delightful land," says the LORD Almighty.* Our nation could be a delightful land. But currently, there is a darkness over America and our communities. We see it every day on the news. A new spirit of tithing in God's people is associated with the blessing of a delightful land.

Malachi 3 also reveals the hearts of those who do not want to tithe. [13] *"You have said harsh things against me," says the LORD. "Yet you ask, 'What have we said against you?'* [14] *"You have said, 'It is futile to serve God.*

What did we gain by carrying out his requirements and going about like mourners before the LORD Almighty? ¹⁵ But now we call the arrogant blessed. Certainly the evildoers prosper, and even those who challenge God escape."'

People who do not want to tithe consider tithing a heavy burden. Their eyes are on the materialistic things in this world. They want to have what others have. They look at the rich and arrogant and call them blessed. They long to be rich with wealth. They do not long to be filled with the Spirit of God. Their "old" nature desires the things of this world more than the things of God. These people must bow before the Lord and ask for His mercy and grace. They need to be filled with the spirit of God so they can turn away from the passions of this world.

Malachi 3 goes on to reveal a people who will do just that. *¹⁶ Then those who feared the LORD talked with each other, and the LORD listened and heard. A scroll of remembrance was written in his presence concerning those who feared the LORD and honored his name.* (Remember part of our honoring God is bringing in the first-fruits from what He has blessed us with) *¹⁷ "They will be mine," says the LORD Almighty, "in the day when I make up my treasured possession. I will spare them, just as in compassion a man spares his son who serves him. ¹⁸ And you will again see the distinction between the righteous and the wicked, between those who serve God and those who do not.*

Will we serve God by bringing in the tithes and offerings? Will our names be written on that scroll as the people who repented and returned to obeying the commands of God carefully?

WORKSHEET FOR CHURCH GOVERNMENT
LIFE TRUTH # 4
THE CHURCH HONORS GOD WITH THEIR TITHES AND OFFERINGS

Question: How should the church view their tithes and offerings?
Answer: The church should honor God by bringing in their tithes and offerings.

Proverbs 3:9-10 (NIV) ⁹ Honor the LORD with your wealth, with the first fruits of all your crops; ¹⁰ then your barns will be filled to overflowing, and your vats will brim over with new wine.

> Write out the Life Truth, question, and answer on one side of an index card and the verse on the other side. Keep it in your Bible for the week. Work on it every day individually and as a family. Have it memorized by next week.

According to Proverbs 3:9-10 What will make our barns overflow?

What does it mean when it says bring in the first fruits?

Read Malachi 3:6-8. What does it say the nation is robbing God of? T_____ and O_____

What is the difference between a tithe and an offering?

Read Deuteronomy 14:28-29. What was the tithe to be used for? L_____
A_____ F_____
W_____

In the end of verse 29 what will the Lord do if we are tithing?

Read Matthew 6:2. What does this verse teach us about our giving?

Read Deuteronomy 15:4-11. How did God design to take care of the poor?

Read Acts 4:32-37. How did the early church view their possessions?

What was the early church selling to meet the needs of people?

Would you be willing to sell something valuable and give the money to meet the needs of others?

Read Acts 5:1-11. Why was the Holy Spirit not pleased with their offering?

Read Mark 12:41-44. How much did the widow give?

What does the widow's offering reveal about her trust in God?

Based on this LIFE TRUTH what can you do individually and as a family to be more devoted to tithes and offerings? How can you better see the needs of people and not be consumed with your own wants?

CHURCH-GOVERNMENT
LIFE TRUTH # 5
THE CHURCH IS A FAMILY

God designed the family unit to be a powerful force in society and a spiritual foundation for a loving and peaceful world. When families function the way the Bible teaches, they experience many blessings from God. Every family member has specific roles to fulfill. By submitting to God's will, they'll experience the abundant life that God intended for them.

The church is a family. It is also a powerful force in society when it functions as the Bible teaches. *Galatians 6:10 (NIV) [10] Therefore, as we have opportunity, let us do good to all people, especially to those who belong to the **family of believers.*** This passage is not referring to blood relatives. It is referring to those who have become Christians. Peter also referred to the church as the family of God in one of his letters.

The church is made up of many individuals who become one family. Have you ever been to a family reunion? You arrive with your immediate family, but you are related to all of the people at the gathering. The individual families at the reunion make up one big extended family. This is similar to how the church comes together. We accept Christ as our Lord and Savior individually. Then we come together to form a church family. Hopefully, our biological family is saved and a part of the church family as well, but even if they are not, we can be a part of God's family. When we receive Christ as our Lord, we are born again into God's family. *John 1:12-13 (NIV) [12] Yet to all who received him, to those who believed in his name, he gave the right to become children of God— [13] children born not of natural descent, nor of human decision or a husband's will, but born of God.*

Do you have fond memories of your family? Special vacations, special moments, special holidays, and special times with those that you love? Do you have heart-breaking memories? Sad memories, let-downs, tragedies, abuse, neglect? Usually, we have both types of memories on many different levels. Hopefully, most of our memories are positive ones and the bad ones are almost forgotten.

Our church family is the same. We have both positive and negative memories. Issues arise when we join a church and expect everyone to behave perfectly. We are all sinners; still in the process of being made holy. Therefore we get offended, bothered, irritated, annoyed, and at times, frustrated, when members of our church family do not act the way we think they should. But we also get blessed, encouraged, lifted up, and supported by them as well.

Have you ever wondered if your church family was functioning perfectly until you joined them? I say this sarcastically, of course, but to drive the point home that we all bring issues into the family. The important truth to realize is that we are family. A family is supposed to stick together, help one another, serve each other, always protect, always hope, and always persevere.

We have way too many people jumping from one local church to the next trying to find the perfect family. The perfect family is nonexistent here on this earth. We must figure out which local family God has called us to and commit to serving its members. Spiritual growth is to begin with our biological family. The church family then becomes our support group for continued growth.

The biological family has structure and roles to fulfill. Fathers are the protectors, providers, and educators. The husband is to be the head of the family and the wife is to be his helpmate. They form one body. The wife is to manage the home and help raise the righteous. Children are to respect and honor their parents as they learn how to obey authority and live righteous lives in society.

The church is to be structured as well. It is to be an orderly place for worship. Paul gives instructions on how the church should worship together in *I Corinthians 14:40 (NIV)* [40] *But everything should be done in a fitting and orderly way.*

He also writes to the church at Colosse in *Colossians 2:5 (NIV)* [5] *For though I am absent from you in body, I am present with you in spirit and delight to see how orderly you are and how firm your faith in Christ is.*

RESPONSIBILITIES OF THE CHURCH

Just as the family has responsibilities; so does the church. Just as a family struggles and suffers when they do not live according to the Scriptures; so does the church. It is important for us to learn God's Word and apply God's principles to our lives. The church is to be a safeguard in society and God's institution to help keep us on the narrow path.

This is a great mission statement for the local church: Acts 2:42-47 (NIV) *42 They devoted themselves to the apostles' teaching and to the fellowship, to the breaking of bread and to prayer. 43 Everyone was filled with awe, and many wonders and miraculous signs were done by the apostles. 44 All the believers were together and had everything in common. 45 Selling their possessions and goods, they gave to anyone as he had need. 46 Every day they continued to meet together in the temple courts. They broke bread in their homes and ate together with glad and sincere hearts, 47 praising God and enjoying the favor of all the people. And the Lord added to their number daily those who were being saved.*

1. MEET WEEKLY

The church family is to have weekly reunions in honor of Christ. These are called worship services. They are held on the Lord's Day, which is Sunday.

Acts 20:7 (NIV) ⁷ On the first day of the week we came together to break bread.

A person who says they are a Christian, but doesn't have a desire to attend a local church is most likely not a part of God's family. Being truly born again gives you a love for people that you've never experienced before. Christians are drawn by the Holy Spirit to love others and not live isolated lives. It is impossible to be a lone-ranger Christian. Christians need each other for accountability, support, and encouragement. It says in *Hebrews 10:25 (NIV) ²⁵ Let us not give up meeting together, as some are in the habit of doing, but let us encourage one another–and all the more as you see the Day approaching.*

2. STUDY THE WORD

Acts tells us that the church devoted themselves to the Apostles teaching. As we learned in our Self Government Life Truth, Scripture alone is what governs us. We need to be like the Bereans and examine the Scriptures every day. *Acts 17:11 (NIV) ¹¹ Now the Bereans were of more noble character than the Thessalonians, for they received the message with great eagerness and examined the Scriptures every day to see if what Paul said was true.*

The church is to be studying the Word of God and applying it in their lives. The church has teachers and preachers, but every individual is responsible to test what is being said. Just as the Bereans examined what Paul said to see if it was true.

3. WORSHIP JESUS

When we get to heaven, we will be worshiping Jesus for all eternity. Until the Lord comes back or calls us home, we need to be praising Jesus individually and as a church. We need to be singing and worshiping together. Paul tells the church to sing in *I Corinthians 14:26 (NIV)* *26 What then shall we say, brothers? When you come together, everyone has a hymn, or a word of instruction, a revelation, a tongue or an interpretation. All of these must be done for the strengthening of the church.*

4. BRING IN OUR TITHES AND OFFERINGS

It is important to bring in our tithes and offerings to honor God and help support the mission of the church. *I Corinthians 16:2 (NIV)* *2 On the first day of every week, each one of you should set aside a sum of money in keeping with his income, saving it up, so that when I come no collections will have to be made.*

5. PRAY

Jesus told us that he wanted his house to be a house of prayer. *Matthew 21:13 (NIV)* *13 "It is written," he said to them, "'My house will be called a house of prayer, but you are making it a den of robbers.'"*

6. MAKE DISCIPLES

Making disciples is both evangelizing those who are not Christians and teaching those who are saved. *Acts 1:8 (NIV) [8] But you will receive power when the Holy Spirit comes on you; and you will be my witnesses in Jerusalem, and in all Judea and Samaria, and to the ends of the earth."*

Matthew 28:17-20 (NIV) [17] When they saw him, they worshiped him; but some doubted. [18] Then Jesus came to them and said, "All authority in heaven and on earth has been given to me. [19] Therefore go and make disciples of all nations, baptizing them in the name of the Father and of the Son and of the Holy Spirit, [20] and teaching them to obey everything I have commanded you. And surely I am with you always, to the very end of the age."

It is the church's responsibility to help others grow in their relationship with Christ. Studying God's Word with your family and other believers is vital to the growth of a church. The passage in Acts says that they devoted themselves to the Apostles' teaching. They met every day together as well as in their homes. They were committed to knowing Christ and applying His teachings to their lives. Is the church today committed to God's Word like it should be? The answer is no. The church needs to return to memorizing and studying God's Word faithfully so its members can share it with others.

If you have participated in the Life Truths from the beginning, you've already learned 25 Life Truths that you can share with others about following Christ. At the end of this study, you will know 40 Life Truths on how to live Christ-centered, productive lives.

7. TAKE CARE OF THOSE IN NEED

The family is responsible for the healthcare of those in their immediate family. When a person has no family left to take care of them, the church is responsible to care for them. *I Timothy 5:9-10 (NIV) ⁹ No widow may be put on the list of widows unless she is over sixty, has been faithful to her husband, ¹⁰ and is well known for her good deeds, such as bringing up children, showing hospitality, washing the feet of the saints, helping those in trouble and devoting herself to all kinds of good deeds.*

The term "list of widows" refers to those the church would support financially because they have no immediate family to care for them. The church is also told to care for the orphans and to remember the poor and the less fortunate in their community. Jesus spent a lot of time with the sinners, drunkards and gluttons. Not just giving things to them but teaching them how to be saved and walk in righteousness. We are to do the same in the community that God has called us to.

THE CHURCH HAS LEADERS

The family is structured with leadership. This helps with the peace and order of a home. The church is to have leaders who support the body and fulfill God's purposes for the church. The leaders have responsibilities to fulfill in the church. When the leaders and the members are fulfilling their purposes, the church becomes a lighthouse in the community.

LEADERS OF THE CHURCH MUST SET A GODLY EXAMPLE

The leaders in the church are to be chosen or appointed. They are to be people of godly character who set an example of walking with Christ. The following passage in Acts shows how the early church chose its leaders. *Acts 6:1-4 (NIV) [1] In those days when the number of disciples was increasing, the Grecian Jews among them complained against the Hebraic Jews because their widows were being overlooked in the daily distribution of food. [2] So the Twelve gathered all the disciples together and said, "It would not be right for us to neglect the ministry of the word of God in order to wait on tables. [3] Brothers, choose seven men from among you who are known to be full of the Spirit and wisdom. We will turn this responsibility over to them [4] and will give our attention to prayer and the ministry of the word."*

Notice that the church was not choosing men to preach or teach, but to serve food to the widows. The twelve Apostles did not ask the church for volunteers. They asked the church to choose seven men who were known to be full of the Holy Spirit and wisdom. Leaders in the church, no matter what level they serve, are to be people full of the Holy Spirit and wisdom. Whether they are cleaning the church, waiting on tables, or preaching the Word, they need to be godly examples.

This should be a challenge to all of us. We should take seriously our character and the example that we are setting forth. The church loses its effectiveness in the community when it does not raise up righteous leaders. Righteous leaders set the example. They stand up against injustices, defend the cause of the helpless, point out sin, and encourage people to follow Christ. The main goal of the church is to transform lives by becoming more like Christ. Therefore, the church should have leaders who model the character of Christ in their lives.

The church should be run by elders or bishops. The Bible sometimes calls these men overseers. These men are responsible for the health of the body. They are to be aware of any false teachings. They are to be acquainted with their members in order to instruct and discipline them if necessary. They, of course, need to be men of integrity and godly character. If you were signing your child up to play a sport you would expect the leader or coach to know something about that sport. You would most likely not sign your son up for football if you knew the teacher was only trained in ballet. Leaders need to have knowledge, experience, and the ability to teach others. This is what God expects as we choose our leaders in the church.

1 Timothy 3:1-15 (NIV) [1] Here is a trustworthy saying: If anyone sets his heart on being an overseer, he desires a noble task. [2] Now the overseer must be above reproach, the husband of but one wife, temperate, self-controlled, respectable, hospitable, able to teach, [3] not given to drunkenness, not violent but gentle, not quarrelsome, not a lover of money. [4] He must manage his own family well and see that his children obey him with proper respect. [5] (If anyone does not know how to manage his own family, how can he take care of God's church?) [6] He must not be a recent convert, or he may become conceited and fall under the same judgment as the devil. [7] He must also have a good reputation with outsiders, so that he will not fall into disgrace and into the devil's trap.

Other leaders that serve in the church are called deacons. The Scripture has qualifications for them as well. *[8] Deacons, likewise, are to be men worthy of respect, sincere, not indulging in much wine, and not pursuing dishonest gain. [9] They must keep hold of the deep truths of the faith with a clear conscience. [10] They must first be tested; and then if there is nothing against them, let them serve as deacons. [11] In the same way, their wives are to be women worthy of respect, not malicious talkers but temperate and trustworthy in everything. [12] A deacon must be the husband of but one wife and must manage his children and his household well. [13] Those who have served well gain an excellent standing and great assurance in their faith in Christ Jesus. ¹⁴ Although I hope to come to you soon, I am writing you these instructions so that, ¹⁵ if I am delayed, you will know how people ought to conduct themselves in God's household, which is the church of the living God, the pillar and foundation of the truth.*

Paul writes these guidelines so that we will know how to conduct ourselves in the church. We are to be a pillar and the foundation of the truth. We should not have men or women leading in the church who are living immoral lifestyles. The Scripture is clear as to the qualifications of our leaders.

The leaders of the church need to administer the Lord's Supper and baptism. They need to protect from the heresies that come up in each generation. They need to administer church discipline when necessary. They need to be the best caretakers they can be with Christ's family.

ADMONISHMENT FOR THE CHURCH
DON'T ACCEPT SIN

The family and the church becomes unhealthy when it accepts sin as the norm. Sin is powerful and very destructive. Unhealthy families accept sin as being a part of who people are. The responsibility of a family is to train in righteousness. If a member of the family has an ungodly characteristic, it is not to be accepted as the norm. For example: If you had a child that was caught lying, you should teach the child that lying is a sin and has destructive consequences. You should not accept lying as a part of who that child is.

By reviewing our self-government responsibilities, we can see if we are being obedient in what the Lord has called us to. Are we serving, praising, encouraging, witnessing, forgiving, being holy, and working? We all have short-comings in some of these areas, but it is the responsibility of the family and the church to encourage one another toward perfection. Paul tells us to aim for perfection in 2 Corinthians 13:11 (NIV)
*11 Finally, brothers, good-by. **Aim for perfection**, listen to my appeal, be of one mind, live in peace. And the God of love and peace will be with you.*

A church family is not to accept sin as the norm either. If someone is living an immoral lifestyle or has an ungodly characteristic, we are to correct, rebuke, encourage, train, and help them out of the sin. To accept the sin brings destruction in the family and the church. We accept sin when we ignore it and don't do anything about it. Sin brings consequences. It needs to be dealt with. We wouldn't just let a nasty infection continue to spread on our leg. We would get medicine and deal with the issue. We must do the same with sin in our lives. Sin grows. It becomes infectious. It is contagious. It is deadly.

Church members who are living in sin need to realize that they are not just bringing consequences on themselves. They are bringing consequences on their entire church family. Sin infects and destroys.

We are to confront sin. We are to ask the hard questions. We must be intentional in helping people. The church fails when we pretend to not see the sin. Paul tells the church in Corinth of the dangers of accepting sin in *I Corinthians 5:6-8 (NIV) [6] Your boasting is not good. Don't you know that a **little yeast** works through the whole batch of dough? [7] Get rid of the old yeast that you may be a new batch without yeast–as you really are. For Christ, our Passover lamb, has been sacrificed. [8] Therefore let us keep the Festival, not with the old yeast, the yeast of malice and wickedness, but with bread without yeast, the bread of sincerity and truth.*

The old yeast is our sinful flesh. The new yeast is the power of Christ in us to be free from sin. Paul warns that even a little yeast will ruin the whole batch. Christ died on the cross and set us free from our sins. Paul goes on to say that if a person, who calls themselves a Christian, is not willing to get help and get out of the sin then we are not to associate with them. *I Corinthians 5:9-13 (NIV) [9] I have written you in my letter not to associate with sexually immoral people– [10] not at all meaning the people of this world who are immoral, or the greedy and swindlers, or idolaters. In that case you would have to leave this world. [11] But now I am writing you that you must not associate with anyone who calls himself a brother but is sexually immoral or greedy, an idolater or a slanderer, a drunkard or a swindler. With such a man do not even eat. [12] What business is it of mine to judge those outside the church? Are you not to judge those inside? [13] God will judge those outside. "Expel the wicked man from among you."*

Paul is not talking about associating with the people in the world. He is referring to the people who call themselves children of God but do not want to repent. A person who calls themselves a Christian and yet walks in darkness is a liar. John says in *1 John 1:6-7 (NIV) ⁶ If we claim to have fellowship with him yet walk in the darkness, we lie and do not live by the truth. ⁷ But if we walk in the light, as he is in the light, we have fellowship with one another, and the blood of Jesus, his Son, purifies us from all sin.*

A biological family and a church family must heed these warnings carefully. For us to accept a sinful lifestyle into our family is to bring the name of Christ into disrepute. By accepting sin, we are blaspheming the name of Christ.

Jude warns of churches that turn the grace of God into a license for sin. *Jude 1:3-4 (NIV) ³ Dear friends, although I was very eager to write to you about the salvation we share, I felt I had to write and urge you to contend for the faith that was once for all entrusted to the saints. ⁴ For certain men whose condemnation was written about long ago have secretly slipped in among you. They are godless men, who change the grace of our God into a license for immorality and deny Jesus Christ our only Sovereign and Lord.*

The grace of God is not a covering for us to live in sin. The grace of God that brings salvation is the power for us to live free from sin. *Titus 2:11-12 (NIV) ¹¹ For the grace of God that brings salvation has appeared to all men. ⁱ² It teaches us to say "No" to ungodliness and worldly passions, and to live self-controlled, upright and godly lives in this present age,*

We have guidelines for those we need to dissociate with because of the sins they refuse to repent of. Many times we do not need to dissociate with a believer. Instead, we need to engage them with the Word and help them grow in Christ.

If you had a son who went out and stole from others, that son would be bringing your reputation into disrepute. We do the same with Christ's name when we allow sin to reign in our lives, our family, or the church. When we accept Christ, we are born into his family. We take on his name and we represent his character. Christian families and churches must take a stand and expel sin from among them. The goal is not to just kick people out. It is to warn them of the seriousness of their sin. If they do not repent, they will have no chance of entering into heaven. It is evident that we are in Christ's family when we display his character in our lives. Jesus says that those who do the will of God are the ones who are a part of His family.

Jesus also warned that when people begin to join his family, divisions will arise in biological families. *Luke 12:51-53 (NIV) ⁵¹ Do you think I came to bring peace on earth? No, I tell you, but division. ⁵² From now on there will be five in one family divided against each other, three against two and two against three. ⁵³ They will be divided, father against son and son against father, mother against daughter and daughter against mother, mother-in-law against daughter-in-law and daughter-in-law against mother-in-law."*

The division is because of their faith in Christ. Some will be non-believers that are against those that have accepted Christ. Some will be those that have accepted Christ but are refusing to repent of their sin and walk in the light.

Look at what Jesus said about those who are a part of his family. *Matthew 12:49-50 (NIV) ⁴⁹ Pointing to his disciples, he said, "Here are my mother and my brothers. ⁵⁰ For whoever does the will of my Father in heaven is my brother and sister and mother."* Those who do the will of God are in Christ's family.

BE DEVOTED TO THE FELLOWSHIP

God has gifted the church with many different gifts. Together we form one body. *Romans 12:4-5 (NIV) ⁴ Just as each of us has one body with many members, and these members do not all have the same function, ⁵ so in Christ **we who are many form one body**, and **each member belongs** to all the others.*

An arm without a hand is not as effective or productive as when they are connected and working together. A leg without a foot has similar struggles. God has designed the body to meet each other's needs and to support one another. Together we accomplish so much more.

2 Corinthians 8:14-15 (NIV) [14] *At the present time your plenty will supply what they need, so that in turn their plenty will supply what you need. Then there will be equality,* [15] *as it is written: "He who gathered much did not have too much, and he who gathered little did not have too little."*

The one who gathers much must learn to help another. The one who gathers little must learn to trust God by allowing others to help out. God designed this situation to grow both.

God puts us in situations where we need to lean on one another. God also allows us to go through hard times to teach us or to help mold us. This is an important issue because many times we are not devoted to one another. Being devoted means that we stick through the good and the bad times together. We don't just brush someone off because we disagree with them. There will be times when we will not agree with someone, but we will still need to be devoted to them and serve them.
Satan loves to divide families, churches, and Christians. He loves to get the "hand" to say it does not need the "arm." He loves to get the "legs" to rebel and run in the opposite direction of the body. He loves to divide husbands and wives.

We need to be praying for the short-comings in the lives of those around us. Remember the second church government truth. The church prays. Jesus told us to always pray and not give up. Are we really praying for the one who is struggling? Or are we just pointing it out to others when they fail? Without Christ, none of us would walk in righteousness. If we were struggling with sin, would we want people gossiping about us to others or praying for us and offering us support? We are to love others as we would want to be loved. This devotion to one another takes sacrifice, commitment, time, and patience. Are we willing to be devoted to the body and care for the areas that need attention? Or are we going to pretend that the person struggling is not a part of us? We are one body. When one part suffers, we all suffer.

Remember that God allows hard times for our growth. If we believe the problem is always about someone else, we are deceived. This belief only helps us justify our own sin. It justifies unforgiveness, hateful words, and judgmental attitudes. Why is it that they need to change in order for us to act righteous? The issue we need to face in every situation is to always respond in love.

Be devoted to one another. Do all you can to keep the bond of peace in your home, church, and community. Be committed in the hard times as well as the good. Paul uses the phrase *"bear with each other."* The word *"bear"* refers to something difficult to do. It is often very difficult to forgive others and support those that have offended you personally or by their actions.

Colossians 3:13 (NIV) [13] Bear with each other and forgive whatever grievances you may have against one another. Forgive as the Lord forgave you.

Christ's prayer for His family is that we be one. *John 17:11 (NIV) [11] I will remain in the world no longer, but they are still in the world, and I am coming to you. Holy Father, protect them by the power of your name—the name you gave me—**so that they may be one as we are one.***

What is the design of a marriage? The two will become one flesh. God desires for there to be unity in the home and in the church. Both are to be unified and devoted to one another. Unity is way deeper than just getting along. Unity takes devotion to one another and being committed to one another. *Romans 14:19 (NIV) [19] Let us therefore make every effort to do what leads to peace and to mutual edification.* Edification is the building up of another. The Bible tells us to mutually build each other up. If we are faultfinding, criticizing, gossiping, complaining, and fighting, then we are not mutually edifying one another. We are tearing things down instead of building up unity.

We need to be devoted to peace and unity in the church and the home. When Jesus was on the cross and saw his mother standing there, he told John to care for his mother. *John 19:25-27 (NIV) ²⁵ Near the cross of Jesus stood his mother, his mother's sister, Mary the wife of Clopas, and Mary Magdalene. ²⁶ When Jesus saw his mother there, and the disciple whom he loved standing nearby, he said to his mother, "Dear woman, here is your son," ²⁷ and to the disciple, "Here is your mother." From that time on, this disciple took her into his home.*

Even on the cross, Jesus took care of his immediate family. The fact that he asked John to care for his mother is somewhat unusual. Mary had other children. Why did Jesus ask His disciple John to care for his mother? Why not allow the other biological children to care for her? The gospel of Matthew gives us insight into the names of some of Jesus' brothers and the fact that he even had sisters. *Matthew 13:55-56 (NIV) ⁵⁵ "Isn't this the carpenter's son? Isn't his mother's name Mary, and aren't his brothers James, Joseph, Simon and Judas? ⁵⁶ Aren't all his sisters with us?* So why did Jesus ask John to care for His mother?

The gospel of John reveals to us that His brothers were not believers. *John 7:5 (NIV) ⁵ For even his own brothers did not believe in him.* Jesus overrides the importance of the biological family and raises the church family to a higher level. Jesus wants His mother to be cared for by a Christian. John took Mary into his home and cared for her from then on.

Jesus is revealing to us that we need our church family more than our biological family. We need Christian support, encouragement, accountability, and love in this world. Lost people cannot understand or see spiritual things. They do not make decisions in the best interest of glorifying God. *I Corinthians 15:33 (NIV) ³³ Do not be misled: "Bad company corrupts good character."*

I am not suggesting that a Christian child needs to divorce his parents and move in with a Christian family. The biological family is very important and needs to respect the roles that God created for them. The dad, mom, and children all have specific roles to fulfill. But Jesus showed us that there may be a time when a Christian needs to choose to be with the church family more than the biological family. A perfect example is when he asked John to care for His own mother.

Jesus' brothers eventually came to salvation and became part of the church of Acts. I Corinthians, Chapter 15, tells us that Jesus appeared to his brother James after the resurrection. We are also told that Jesus' brothers were in the prayer meeting on the day of Pentecost. At some point after the resurrection, they became believers. But it is important to understand that when they didn't believe, Jesus chose John to care for His mother. He did not want to put her in the company of unbelievers, even when those unbelievers were his brothers.

As a church family, we need to be looking around for those who do not have a believing parent or parents. We need to be bringing them alongside us and helping them grow. We need to be helping single parents, orphans, widows, and those who have nowhere to go on holidays. We need to be devoted to one another.

ACCEPT ONE ANOTHER

Accept the person you are having issues with. Lay down your rights and serve them. Benefit them. Our job is to gently and lovingly come alongside those who need help. We are to accept one another just as God has accepted us. *Romans 15:7 (NIV)*
[7] Accept one another, then, just as Christ accepted you, in order to bring praise to God.

How did Christ accept you? Did He make you clean yourself off before you were allowed to be a part of His family? Does He turn His back on you and refuse to help you when you are going through an issue? Does He point out all your faults and make you feel bad about your short-comings?

Romans 15:5-6 (NIV) [5] May the God who gives endurance and encouragement give you a spirit of unity among yourselves as you follow Christ Jesus, [6] so that with one heart and mouth you may glorify the God and Father of our Lord Jesus Christ.

Ephesians 4:2-3 (NIV) ² *Be completely humble and gentle; be patient, bearing with one another in love.* ³ *Make every effort to keep the unity of the Spirit through the bond of peace.*

Are we being patient as Christ transforms those around us? Or do we get irritated that they are not perfect? We need to pray for them. We need to be patient with them.

Many times a person joins a church family looking for someone to serve them and meet their needs. But God has called, equipped, and gifted his children to bring ministry to others in a family. We have the responsibility to serve one another. A family is not like a restaurant. A restaurant is where people cook your food, serve your food, and wash your dishes. In a family, we cook the meal, set the table, and wash the dishes together.

You may complain about the service or the food in a restaurant, but you better not complain about the food or the service in your family. If you do, you will bring dissension and disunity. You probably should not complain in either case, but especially in a family. Your focus should be on all the ways you can serve, minister, love, and forgive.

I will close with this passage. It is a passage read at many weddings, but the context is for the church family. Paul tells the church that this is the kind of love they need to have for one another. It is the same kind of love and acceptance that God has for us.

1 Corinthians 13:4-7 (NIV) [4] Love is patient, love is kind. It does not envy, it does not boast, it is not proud. [5] It is not rude, it is not self-seeking, it is not easily angered, it keeps no record of wrongs. [6] Love does not delight in evil but rejoices with the truth. [7] It always protects, always trusts, always hopes, always perseveres.

WORKSHEET FOR CHURCH GOVERNMENT
LIFE TRUTH # 5
THE CHURCH IS A FAMILY

Question: How should the church view its members?
Answer: We should accept one another as God accepts us.

Matthew 12:49-50 (NIV) [49] Pointing to his disciples, he said, "Here are my mother and my brothers. [50] For whoever does the will of my Father in heaven is my brother and sister and mother."

> Write out the Life Truth, question, and answer on one side of an index card and the verse on the other side. Keep it in your Bible for the week. Work on it every day individually and as a family. Have it memorized by next week.

According to Matthew 12:49-50. Why does Jesus call these people His family?

Whoever does what will be included in God's family?

Read Luke 12:51-53. How does Jesus bring division to a family?

Read 1 Corinthians 12:12-26. Who has arranged the parts of the body (v18)?

What is God's goal in putting the body together (v 25)? No D_____ and E_____ C_____.

God joins the members in a marriage and he expects them to become one flesh. He also expects the church family to become unified. Read John 17:20-23. How many are to be one (v20)?
(v23) God wants us to be brought into C_____ U_____.
Unity means no divisions.

Read 1 Peter 4:7-10. What does love cover over? M_____ of S_____.
The opposite of covering over sin is pointing it out, holding a grudge, unforgiveness, and faultfinding. This brings division. We must love and cover over how many sins?

Circle the words or phrases that reflect how God deals with our sin.
Harsh   Unkind   Belittles us   Keeps bringing up our past sins   Lovingly   Gentle   Graciously   Patiently
Which of these characteristics could we grow in more to help promote unity?

Based on this LIFE TRUTH what can you do individually and as a family to be more devoted to one another? God expects us to behave like Christ in all situations. Are there any situations in your life that you need to change to reflect His character?

CHURCH-GOVERNMENT LIFE TRUTH # 6
THE CHURCH IS AGAINST ABORTION

According to Webster's dictionary, abortion is the termination of a pregnancy after, accompanied by, resulting in, or closely followed by the death of the embryo or fetus. Abortion is the number one cause of death in America. (www.prolifecorner.com and www.epm.org). In Missouri, there are over 7000 abortions a year. This is an average of 20 deaths a day.

Ronald Reagan, our 40th US president, wrote a book in 1983 called *Abortion and the Conscience of the Nation*. He states on page 16, *"Make no mistake, abortion-on-demand is not a right granted by the Constitution. No serious scholar, including one disposed to agree with the Court's results* (Roe vs. Wade), *has argued that the framers of the Constitution intended to create such a right."*

The founders intended to protect life and liberty. We see this in the second paragraph of our Declaration of Independence. *"We hold these truths to be self-evident, that all men are created equal, that they are endowed by their Creator with certain unalienable rights that among these are life, liberty and the pursuit of happiness."* We have an unalienable right to life from our creator. God is the creator of life and He decides when a person is to be born and when a person is to die.

This issue of taking the life of a child is nothing new. In an old historical document entitled, *Epistle of Barnabas* it states on page 19.5, *"Killers of the child, who abort the mold of God."* Barnabas goes on to say, *"You shall love your neighbor more than your own life. You shall not slay a child by abortion. You shall not kill that which has already been generated."*

Tertullian said in his apology on page 9.4, *"It does not matter whether you take away a life that is born, or destroy one that is coming to the birth. In both instances, the destruction is murder."*

Augustine in his writings *On Marriage* 1.17.15 warns of the "terrible crime of the murder of an unborn child."

The church in our generation needs to do two things. First, we must realize that many women have had abortions and many lives have been affected by them. We must offer grace and forgiveness to those that are suffering because of this decision. God is a God of forgiveness and restoration. Three websites that offer help to those hurting because of abortion are: www.nationalhelpline.org; www.abortionrecovery.org; www.safehavenministries.com

 Second, we must continue our efforts to get this decision overturned in our nation. We must educate the nation on God's perspective in this matter. We must use the scriptures to make disciples of all nations, teaching them to obey all things that Christ taught.

Since the Supreme Court's ruling in 1973, legalizing abortion across our land, people have sought to reverse the decision. Attempts to completely remove abortion from our land have failed. Small battles have been won and lost, but this must not stop the cry of the church. The church is to be *"the pillar and foundation of the truth"* as Paul states in 1 Timothy 3:15. The church is to stand up against heresies and protect the rights of those who cannot speak for themselves. We must not become lazy, apathetic, or indifferent in our efforts to save unborn children. We must educate and raise a generation who will not stop until they defeat this evil.

On January 23, 2012, Lifesitenews.com presented their analysis. They estimated that since 1973, there have been 54.5 million babies aborted. In my small Missouri town, there are about 7,000 people. This means the amount of abortions since 1973 equals approximately 8,000 small towns in the U.S. being destroyed.

Some may argue that removing "cells" from a pregnant woman is not the same as murder. What does the medical profession use as their standard for "life"? The medical profession says that if you have a detectable heartbeat or brainwave activity you are alive. The cells of an embryo have a heartbeat eighteen days after conception. They have detectable brainwave activity forty days after conception. Abortions generally occur more than 49 days after conception.

Until the new morning after pill, abortions were administered when these "cells" were already considered alive by our own medical professionals. In Missouri Law, Chapter 188.015, regulation of abortion states, *"Abortion: the act of using or prescribing any instrument, device, medicine, drug, or any other means or substance with the intent to destroy the life of an embryo or fetus in his or her mother's womb."* Our own law states that our goal in abortion is to destroy life.

In 1857, the Supreme Court ruled that Negroes were not citizens of the United States. This ruling was part of the Dred Scott case. He eventually won his freedom, but it did not happen overnight. It was a long, hard fought battle. Today, we know the good that came from this decision. All people are created by God and have God-given unalienable rights. A person's race does not matter. People that stand up for the rights of others are heroes. Martin Luther King Jr. and Mother Teresa are just two of the many people who are remembered for their commitment and compassion in defending the rights of others.

Abortion is a terrible evil that opened the door for man to decide when someone should live or die. In

Indiana, there was the case against Baby Doe, a child born with Down Syndrome. Doctors advised the parents to kill the child because he would be retarded and not have good quality of life. The case was taken before the Indiana Supreme Court. The court ruled in favor of the doctors. The child was eventually starved to death. Man has no right to decide who should live and who should die. This is God's decision. Our responsibility is to love God and love our fellowman. Life on this earth is not a matter of convenience or quality, but one of obedience to our creator. We are to love and minister to all people, no matter what issues they must face.

The church should be desperately seeking to overturn the Supreme Court's decision concerning abortion. It is a decision that has greatly affected our entire nation. We should be one voice on this issue. We need to beg God for His forgiveness and protect the gift of life.

What can we say to educate people about abortion?

1. ABORTION IS MURDER

Murder is the intentional taking of human life. The purpose of an abortion is to destroy life. Missouri Law, Chapter 188.015, regulation of abortions states, *"Abortion: the act of using or prescribing any instrument, device, medicine, drug, or any other means or substance with the intent **to destroy the life** of an embryo or fetus in his or her mother's womb."*

Murder is the unlawful killing of a human life. In the Old Testament, the punishment for intentional murder was death. *Exodus 21:12-14 (NIV)* *[12] "Anyone who strikes a man and kills him shall surely be put to death. [13] However, if he does not do it intentionally, but God lets it happen, he is to flee to a place I will designate. [14] But if a man schemes and kills another man deliberately, take him away from my altar and put him to death.* God does not want us to decide who lives and who dies. That is His responsibility.. *I Samuel 2:6 (NIV)* *[6] "The LORD brings death and makes alive; he brings down to the grave and raises up.*

God might allow us to take the life of another, but we will be judged for it. Some may argue that the law says abortion is legal. If the law says that it is okay, then how can it be wrong? Man may legalize sin, but the church is to live by God's law. The sixth commandment of the Ten states in *Exodus 20:13 (NIV)* *[13] "You shall not murder."*

Satan seeks to numb us to reality of death. There are many violent scenes depicting murder on television. There are many video games that depict murder as no big deal. Life is precious. The church needs to respect life and turn off violent shows that depict murder. People become desensitized to violence because they see it over and over again in the media. Why does a teenager walk into a school and start shooting? Why do people continue to kill others? It is because they have become desensitized to the preciousness of life. Violence and murder no longer shock them.

The church must stand up for life. We need to stop watching violent shows. They are not innocent entertainment. Satan has a goal. He is achieving his goal when we allow these images into our homes and lives. We must be more concerned with pleasing God than pleasing ourselves. Would Jesus watch violent shows that depict murder? Every life is precious to God. It breaks His heart when man, inspired by Satan, murders another.

No matter what the law says, the church is to obey God rather than man; even if man says it is legal to abort a baby. In the New Testament, there was an incident where King Herod committed adultery. He divorced his wife and took his brother's wife for his own. He was the king at the time, so no one went against his decision except a bold man of God, named John the Baptist. While everyone just accepted what he did and kept quiet about it, King Herod heard John boldly speak against it. Herodias was the woman who was his brother's wife and whom Herod married. She hated John for accusing them of sin. It says in *Mark 6:17-18 (NIV)* [17] *For Herod himself had given orders to have John arrested, and he had him bound and put in prison. He did this because of Herodias, his brother Philip's wife, whom he had married.* [18] *For John had been saying to Herod, "It is not lawful for you to have your brother's wife."*

John was not afraid of Herod. He called sin exactly what it was. He said, *"It is not lawful for you to have your brother's wife."* John was referring to God's law; not man's law. Leviticus 18:16 (NIV) ¹⁶ *"'Do not have sexual relations with your brother's wife; that would dishonor your brother.*

We need to be as bold as John on this topic. We need to tell people that abortion is murder. According to God's Word, it is not lawful to allow abortions. Remember our first Self Government Life Truth – Scripture alone is what governs us. What if people persecute you for taking such a stand? John the Baptist was beheaded over the stance that he took. But where is John now? He is in heaven with Jesus. Martin Luther King Jr. was shot and killed for his stance. But where is he today? He is in heaven with Jesus. The people of God need to be bold and not fear man. We need to speak out against abortions. It is murder and God is not pleased with it. God can restore, heal, and forgive those who have had abortions, those who have performed abortions, and those who have allowed abortions to occur; but we must repent now.

1. IT IS A CHILD IN THE WOMB

Many argue that it is only "cells" in the womb. There is a double standard on this topic. If someone kills a pregnant mother, the person is charged with a double homicide.

Advocates for abortion call what is in the womb "cells" in order to justify what they are doing. We know what these "cells" become if left to grow as God intends. It is a child in the womb and not just cells. A child that grows and matures just as God designed. It is the miracle of life.

Our answers do not come from the debate or the reasoning of man. Our answers come from the Scriptures. The Bible has a lot to say about the "child" in the womb.

In the Old Testament there is a story about Jacob and Esau in the womb. Isaac their father is praying to God to allow Rebekah his wife to have children. The Lord answers his prayer and she becomes pregnant. *Genesis 25:21-23 (NIV)* [21] *Isaac prayed to the LORD on behalf of his wife, because she was barren. The LORD answered his prayer, and his wife Rebekah became pregnant.* [22] *The babies jostled each other within her, and she said, "Why is this happening to me?" So she went to inquire of the LORD.* [23] *The LORD said to her, "Two nations are in your womb, and two peoples from within you will be separated; one people will be stronger than the other, and the older will serve the younger."*

Notice that the passage calls what is in her womb babies and not cells. They are babies, and more specifically, they each have a purpose and a plan designed by God. They each will become a nation. We have no right to abort the plans of God. God is the creator of life. We are not to decide who will live and who will die.

Look at this passage in *Matthew 1:18 (NIV)* ¹⁸ *This is how the birth of Jesus Christ came about: His mother Mary was pledged to be married to Joseph, but before they came together, she was found to be with child through the Holy Spirit.*

Even at the very beginning of her pregnancy the Scriptures are calling what is in Mary's womb a child and not "cells." The Bible is clear; beautiful children are in the womb.

A similar reference was made about John the Baptist when he was in his mother's womb. *Luke 1:41 (NIV) ⁴¹ When Elizabeth heard Mary's greeting, the baby leaped in her womb, and Elizabeth was filled with the Holy Spirit.*

They are not cells. They are children that God has created for a purpose.

2. NO ONE IS AN ACCIDENT

One argument that people use to defend abortion is that a woman should have the right to choose what is best for her body. Many say that a woman who is raped should not have to have the child from her rapist. Rape is a terrible evil. Those that do such a heinous crime should be punished. But do we have a right to abort the child?

This was the argument in the Roe vs. Wade case that legalized abortion. Norma McCorvey was the young lady in the trial who claimed to be raped. Later, she admitted that she lied and was manipulated during the trial. The website www.unbornintheusa.org says this, *"Norma McCorvey realizes that in her desperate state she was being used. She had become a legal pawn for the country's thriving abortion industry, and a poster girl for the pro-choice movement. A repentant Norma travels the country speaking out against abortion and has written about her role in Roe vs. Wade in her book, "Won By Love." In it, she reveals how she was never raped, and regrets to say: This means that the abortion case that destroyed every state law protecting the unborn was based on a lie."*

Abortion was legalized on the belief that Norma McCorvey was raped and should not have to carry the baby to full term. Look at the breakdown on why children are aborted:

- 1% are victims of rape
- 1 % had fetal abnormalities
- 4 % had a doctor who said the mother's health would worsen if they continued the pregnancy
- 50 % said they didn't want to be a single parent or they had problems in current relationships
- 66 % stated they could not afford a child
- 75 % said the child would interfere with their lives

How has abortion gone from cases of rape *only* to a matter of convenience? 94% of children aborted are aborted for reasons of convenience. This brings us back to the question of whether we have the right to abort a child even in the case of rape. The Biblical answer is no. God does not create any accidents.

Have you ever heard of James Robinson? He has a television program called Life Today. He and his wife are authors of several books. They have formed many organizations. Organizations to rescue hurting children, drill wells in poor countries, feed the poor, and provide medical care for those who cannot afford it. They have helped hundreds of thousands of people over the years and blessed many more through their ministry. Did you know that Mr. Robison was born out of rape? What if his mother had chosen to abort him? Our world would be a little darker without him and his ministry. God does not make mistakes.

Have you ever heard of Pam Stenzel? She has written several books on the topic of abstinence. She travels the country educating young people on the dangers of premarital sex. She has helped thousands of young people through her message. Did you know that she was born out of rape? She has also authored a book titled, *Except in Cases of Rape*. Her book is the testimonies of many people who have been born out of rape and have gone on to make a difference in society.

God does not create any accidents. He can take a terrible tragedy like rape and turn the situation around by creating a beautiful child who makes a difference in the world.

Look at this passage in *Acts 17:26-28 (NIV)* [26] *From one man he made every nation of men, that they should inhabit the whole earth; and he determined the times set for them and the exact places where they should live.* [27] *God did this so that men would seek him and perhaps reach out for him and find him, though he is not far from each one of us.* [28] *'For in him we live and move and have our being.' As some of your own poets have said, 'We are his offspring.'*

The passage tells us that God determines the exact place and time for us to be born. God chooses to allow some to be born out of cases of rape. Children of rape have a purpose just like the rest of us. We may not like the situation. We may not like the circumstances. But we can trust that God has a good purpose and plan for it all. Remember, it is Satan who causes people to do evil things like rape. It is God who turns things around for His good; like James Robinson, Pam Stenzel and the many others.

3. GOD IS THE CREATOR OF LIFE

God is the creator of us all. He is the one who decides to whom and where we will be born. Look at this passage in *Psalm 139:13-16 (NIV)* [13] *For you created my inmost being; you knit me together in my mother's womb.* ¹⁴ *I praise you because I am fearfully and wonderfully made; your works are wonderful, I know that full well.* ¹⁵ *My frame was not hidden from you when I was made in the secret place. When I was woven together in the depths of the earth,* ¹⁶ *your eyes saw my unformed body. All the days ordained for me were written in your book before one of them came to be.*

The passage speaks of the "cells" of the "unformed body", but it also reminds us that God is the one forming those cells together into a beautiful child. A life that has been specially chosen and with great care created to fulfill the purposes of God. We must not dare to interfere with what the Lord is doing. We must treat everyone with the greatest respect for we are all made in the image of God.

The passage lets us know that all of our days are ordained, even before we are born, we are written in God's book. God is the author of life. The opposite of life is death. When a person is dead they cease to move. They have no life in them and therefore they cannot move. God is the giver of life. The evidence that we are alive is that we are moving, breathing, and functioning. It says in Acts 17:25 (NIV) ²⁵ *And he is not served by human hands, as if he needed anything, because he himself gives all men life and breath and everything else.* When the "cells" are moving, growing, and maturing inside the mother's body, we know that they are alive. God is the creator of life. It is because of him that we live and move and have our being.

4. GOD IS A GOD OF FORGIVENESS

For those that have had abortions and those that have performed abortions, God offers forgiveness. God longs for us to ask Him for forgiveness and to come to Him in repentance. If you have been a part of an abortion, cry out to God for forgiveness and let Him heal you. He died on the cross for all sin. When we confess our sin, He purifies us. I John 1:9 (NIV)
[9] If we confess our sins, he is faithful and just and will forgive us our sins and purify us from all unrighteousness.

Those who have not stood up to protect the unborn also need to seek the Lord's forgiveness. The Scriptures are clear that we are responsible to speak up and defend those who are defenseless, weak, and innocent. There is no one more defenseless than an unborn child. Where is the cry to defend the unborn?

The nation of Israel was accused of having a lot of blood on their hands because they did not speak up for the weak. Could the same be said of our generation? Could the same be said of you? *Isaiah 1:15-17 (NIV) [15] When you spread out your hands in prayer, I will hide my eyes from you; even if you offer many prayers, I will not listen. Your hands are full of blood; [16] wash and make yourselves clean. Take your evil deeds out of my sight! Stop doing wrong, [17] learn to do*

right! Seek justice, encourage the oppressed. Defend the cause of the fatherless, plead the case of the widow.
It says in *Psalm 82:3-4 (NIV)* ³ *Defend the cause of the weak and fatherless; maintain the rights of the poor and oppressed.* ⁴ *Rescue the weak and needy; deliver them from the hand of the wicked.*

The innocent, defenseless children need to be rescued. Here are some facts about abortions and how these babies are killed. It is hard to read, but it needs to be told. This information was taken from www.gospelway.com/morality/abortion.php.

D & C or Dilatation and Curettage Abortion

This method is common during the first 13 weeks of pregnancy. A tiny hoe-like instrument, the curette, is inserted into the womb through the dilated cervix. The abortionist then scrapes the wall of the uterus, cutting the baby's body to pieces.

Suction Abortion

This technique, pioneered in Communist China, is common for early pregnancies. A powerful suction tube is inserted into the womb; then the body of the developing baby is torn to pieces and sucked into a jar. Even early in pregnancy body parts are recognizable as arms, legs, etc. There is ultra-sound evidence that the baby feels the pain (as in the movie "The Silent Scream").

Salt Poisoning

This has been used in advanced pregnancies. A needle is inserted through the mother's abdomen, and a strong salt solution is injected into the amniotic fluid that surrounds the child. The baby is slowly poisoned and burned by the salt it swallows and "breathes." The mother then goes into labor and expels a grotesque, shriveled baby. Some babies are born alive but deformed.

Hysterotomy or Cesarean Section Abortion

This method is used in the last trimester of pregnancy. The womb is entered by surgery. Then the tiny baby is killed and removed.

Prostaglandin Chemical Abortion

Hormone-like compounds are injected into the muscle of the uterus, causing it to contract intensely and push out the developing baby. Many babies are born alive.

Dilatation & Extraction ("Partial Birth Abortion")

In this late-term method, the doctor uses forceps to remove the baby from the womb. The head, however, is too big to be extracted. So the abortionist cuts a hole in the base of the skull, suctions out the brain, crushes the skull, and then removes the baby. (See *Lake County Right-to-Life Newsletter*, 4&5/93.)

Newer methods include the "morning after" pill, which may allow conception and then causes the fertilized egg to be expelled from the womb. Note that many so-called "contraceptives" (such as the I.U.D. and even some forms of the "pill") may have a similar effect. Ask your doctor how a "contraceptive" works before using it.

(The above information is taken from "Abortion: What It Is," *A.L.L. About Issues*, July, 1982, and other sources.)

Andy Andrews wrote a book entitled, *How Do You Kill 11,000,000 People?* The book is about the terrible tragedy in Germany when Adolf Hitler led his army to kill 11,283,000 people between 1933 and 1945. This figure only represents the institutionalized killings and not the many who were killed during World War II. He answers the question throughout the book and comes to a few conclusions. First, you lie to the people. Second, you tell them the lie over and over until the people believe it. Third, the tragedy continues when good people choose to do nothing. Mr. Andrews tells a chilling story from an eyewitness. This witness was a church member. The train tracks that carried many to their death ran right behind his church.

The story on page 39 reads, "*We heard stories of what was happening to the Jews, but we tried to distance ourselves from it, because we felt, what could anyone do to stop it? Each Sunday morning, we would hear the train whistle blowing in the distance, then the wheels coming over the tracks. We became disturbed when we heard cries coming from the train as it passed by. We realized that it was carrying Jews like cattle in the cars! Week after week the whistle would blow. We dreaded to hear the sounds of those wheels because we knew that we would hear the cries of the Jews en route to a death camp. Their screams tormented us.*"

The tragedy that happened in Germany did not happen because people did not know what was going on. It was because people were afraid to stand up against the injustice. In Germany, you could be thrown into the camp and killed for speaking out against Hitler and what he was doing.

The eyewitness continues on page 40, "*We knew the time the train was coming and when we heard the whistle blow we began singing hymns. By the time the train came past our church, we were singing at the top of our voices. If we heard the screams, we sang more loudly and soon we heard them no more. Years passed and no one talks about it now, but I still hear that train whistle in my sleep.*"

We read this story with tears and wonder how could they not do anything? Why did they just sing louder and ignore what was happening in their town? In

159

Germany, they had the fear of death, torture, and being torn from their families. We have nothing to fear in comparison. We need to be speaking out against the injustice of abortion. We need to protect and defend the unborn babies that are being killed in our nation every week. We need to be appalled that our government spends roughly $540 million dollars a year to destroy children; calling it healthcare. It is estimated that 54 million children have been aborted since 1973. This number is hard to even comprehend but it is a reality in today's world. What will we do? Will we continue to sing our church songs and ignore what's going on around us?

We need people to fill church prayer meetings. We need to beg God for forgiveness and to ask Him to heal our land. Our nation is falling apart because people are too busy to come to church and pray. We must not be too busy to pray. We need people to speak out against abortion by calling their state representatives, by being aware of new legislation, and by lobbying for laws to be changed. Abortion needs to be banned from our nation. We need to elect candidates who believe in the Scriptures and agree that abortion is murder.

We need healing groups for those that have had abortions and Bible studies and other ministries to help those who are hurting because of a decision to abort. The church needs to minister and offer forgiveness to those affected by this sin.

God is a God of forgiveness, but we must repent. We must ask Him to forgive us and to help us get the evil of abortion out of our land. Every life is a gift from God. Life is to be cherished, nurtured, and protected.

What is God leading you to do?

WORKSHEET FOR CHURCH GOVERNMENT
LIFE TRUTH # 6
THE CHURCH IS AGAINST ABORTION

Question: How should the church view life?
Answer: Every life is sacred and God chooses where and when a person is to be born.

Acts 17:26,27 (NIV) ²⁶ From one man he made every nation of men, that they should inhabit the whole earth; and he determined the times set for them and the exact places where they should live. ²⁷ God did this so that men would seek him and perhaps reach out for him and find him, though he is not far from each one of us.

> Write out the Life Truth, question, and answer on one side of an index card and the verse on the other side. Keep it in your Bible for the week. Work on it every day individually and as a family. Have it memorized by next week.

Read Acts 17:24-31. To be alive is to be moving. To be dead is unable to move, breath, or think.

According to verse 25 who gives all men life?
Who decided who our parents will be, when, and where we will be born? (v 26)

What is God's purpose in choosing our parents, place, and time to be born? (v 27)

What must everyone do to be saved? (v 30)

Read Psalm 139:13-16. Where were we when God was knitting us together? (v 13)

Some people say that the "cells" inside a pregnant mother are not a person, but what does God's word say about the unformed body? (v 16) Circle the answer: Person   or   Cells

Read Jeremiah 1:5. When did God appoint Jeremiah as a prophet? (Before or after his birth?)

What does this tells us about every life that God creates?

Read Genesis 30:22-24. Who opens wombs and places life inside mothers?

If God opens the womb and creates a life should a person destroy it?   Why not?

If a woman becomes pregnant and she does not abort her child what will happen 9 months later?

Read Exodus 20:13. Murder is the intentional taking of human life. If a woman aborts her baby what is she doing?

Read Acts 13:38; John 8:2-11. Does God want to forgive those who have had abortions?

Based on this LIFE TRUTH, what can you do individually and as a family to be more active in the fight against abortion? Is God leading you to be a leader in this fight? What is He calling you to do?

CHURCH-GOVERNMENT LIFE TRUTH # 7
THE CHURCH HONORS MARRIAGE

The Scriptures tell us that we are to honor marriage. To honor means to recognize the value and the importance of a person or a thing. *Hebrews 13:4 (NIV) [4] Marriage should be honored by all, and the marriage bed kept pure, for God will judge the adulterer and all the sexually immoral.*

The opposite of honor is disgrace. The church was designed to honor the institution of marriage by being an example of holy living. However, even the church in this generation has brought disgrace to the institution of marriage. The current divorce, immorality, and pornography rates in the church are disgraceful. Today's church needs to repent and honor the institution of marriage once again.
As parents, when our children do something that can harm them, we try to stop them. We discipline them and strive to change their behavior for the betterment of themselves and society. What if your child stole candy out of the candy jar and lied about it? As godly parents, we would discipline them and tell them about the consequences of their behavior if didn't change.

Current consequences refer to appropriate and immediate discipline that the child would receive.

Future consequences are the different types of punishment the child might face later on in life. When we do not honor marriage as God intended, we bring current and future consequences upon ourselves and our nation. Unfortunately, this is what is happening to us today. Our culture is seeking to redefine marriage as no longer being just between one man and one woman. The church is as much to blame as anyone else. How can the church be to blame? The church can be blamed because it has repeatedly neglected the institution of marriage. It has allowed marriage to be centered around an individual's self-fulfillment instead of being about glorifying God.

Our hedonistic society is focused on self-pleasure rather than being obedient to the God who created us. This selfish mindset has entered the church. Many people simply do not understand the importance of honoring marriage and keeping the marriage bed pure. When we make marriage about self-fulfillment instead of glorifying God, we begin to redefine its roles and responsibilities.
In this generation, if we do not feel like being married, we get a divorce. If we do not feel like waiting until our wedding day to consummate our marriage, we indulge ourselves and think nothing of the consequences.

This hedonistic living in the church has caused our light to grow dim. Today's church has many people suffering from depression, anxiety, confusion, and mistrust because of our disobedience. The "salt" is not preserving our nation from moral decay. Instead, we have become a part of the decay. If marriage is only about self-fulfillment, then why **not** change it to mean different things for different people? Society has seen our bad witness and is confused and looking for answers.

The church must repent. We must return to honoring marriage and become an example to the world around us. God promises to bless nations that obey Him.

Today the average age to marry is 27. Since people are waiting longer to get married cohabitation rates are up. Many of the couples that cohabitate before marriage end up in divorce. Sexual immorality rates are up as well. Two-thirds of the women who have a child by the age of 30 are not married. Forty-eight percent of all first births in America are to unmarried women.

In 1970, premarital births to women in their 20's were an exception to the norm. Today, women in their 20's who have a child out of wedlock are in the majority. (This information was from an article in the AFA Journal, September 2013, titled *When's the Right Time to Marry?*) This fast decline in society is alarming. Our nation is in such a moral decline that the Supreme Court recently ruled in favor of same sex unions. We may be shocked about this ruling, but how many people do you know living in an immoral relationship? Whether they are cohabitating, having relations before marriage, or have divorced and remarried another; moral decay didn't happened all at once.

We have eaten the *candy* that God told us not to taste until marriage and we are experiencing the consequences. We have not waited and shown godly restraint. We have indulged in our own pleasures without considering the effects of our sin. How can we repent and turn this nation around? It must start with each individual asking God for forgiveness and for the church to return to a commitment of honoring the marriage bed.

Let's look at some specific ways that we dishonor marriage.

WAYS WE DISHONOR MARRIAGE

1. Adultery

Adultery is when a member of a marriage union decides to have relations with someone other than their spouse. We learned in the Family Government Life Truth that marriage is to be between one man and one woman. The New Testament gives only three reasons to dissolve a marriage union; adultery, death and an unbelieving spouse leaving the relationship.

Our society used to recognize adultery as a sin. People understood what God said about it in His Word. The Ten Commandments were posted in our public schools and on our courthouses to remind us of His laws. The seventh commandment tells us in Exodus 20:14 *(NIV)*[14] *"You shall not commit adultery."*

Many people do not even know that marrying another person, after having an unscriptural divorce, is committing adultery. Jesus spoke on this topic in *Matthew 5:31-32 (NIV)* [31] *"It has been said, 'Anyone who divorces his wife must give her a certificate of divorce.'* [32] *But I tell you that anyone who divorces his wife, except for marital unfaithfulness, causes her to become an adulteress, and anyone who marries the divorced woman commits adultery.*

Notice this passage and the meaning of it. Jesus says that if someone divorces their spouse for irreconcilable differences and then marries another, they commit adultery. This causes the woman to be an adulterous.

Many marriages, across our country and even in the church, are being dissolved for irreconcilable differences instead of for Biblical reasons. The marriage union is to be held in high regard. It is not to be easily broken. Why are people divorcing? They are divorcing because the other person is not meeting their needs. They are consumed with the pleasure of self. They are not consumed with the glory of God.

Paul gives us more insight into what Christ taught on this topic in *1 Corinthians 7:10-11 (NIV)*
[10] To the married I give this command (not I, but the Lord): A wife must not separate from her husband. [11] But if she does, she must remain unmarried or else be reconciled to her husband. And a husband must not divorce his wife.

If you separate or divorce from your spouse and it is not with a Biblical basis, you are not free to remarry. Remember, if you remarry you will be committing adultery.

Later on in Jesus' ministry some Pharisees wanted Jesus to clarify His beliefs on divorce. *Matthew 19:3-10 (NIV) [3] Some Pharisees came to him to test him. They asked, "Is it lawful for a man to divorce his wife for any and every reason?" [4] "Haven't you read," he replied, "that at the beginning the Creator 'made them male and female,' [5] and said, 'For this reason a man will leave his father and mother and be united to his wife, and the two will become one flesh'? [6] So they are no longer two, but one. Therefore what God has joined together, let man not separate." [7] "Why then," they asked, "did Moses command that a man give his wife a certificate of divorce and send her away?" [8] Jesus replied, "Moses permitted you to divorce your wives because your hearts were hard. But it was not this way from the beginning. [9] I tell you that anyone who divorces his wife, except for marital unfaithfulness, and marries another woman commits adultery." [10] The disciples said to him, "If this is the situation between a husband and wife, it is better not to marry."*

In this passage, we learn that the institution is to be between one man and one woman. We can also see the sacred commitment of the marriage vow. The disciples understood what Jesus was saying when they said, *"If this is the situation between a husband and wife, it is better not to marry."*

2. Fornication

Fornication is any sexual immorality. The Bible approves of sexual activity only when it is between a man and a woman within the marriage union. Sex before marriage, sex outside the bonds of marriage, homosexual activity, and prostitution are all acts of fornication.

Moral depravity increases as our standards lower in society. A nation doesn't wake up one day and find out that their Supreme Court has ruled in favor of same sex unions. The decay began years before this decision was made. The church is partly to blame. After all, we are to be the "light" to push back the darkness. We are to be the "salt" that preserves the nation from decay.

Sexual immorality has been around since the fall of man. Jesus said in *Matthew 15:19-20 (NIV)* [19] *For out of the heart come evil thoughts, murder, adultery, sexual immorality, theft, false testimony, slander.* [20] *These are what make a man 'unclean'; but eating with unwashed hands does not make him 'unclean.'"*

Our sinful natures are prone to commit sexual immorality. If left to ourselves, we engage in our sinful desires. Only in Christ, can we be overcomers and walk in righteousness. The danger is when we move the standard of moral purity. Many young people in the church today believe that sex before marriage is not a sin. They have lowered God's standards and have become participants in the slippery slope of moral decay.

The Scriptures enlighten us to the dangers of such a tragedy in society. Paul speaks about a time when God's people slipped into sexual immorality. Judgment eventually fell upon them because they had lowered God's standards of holiness. *I Corinthians 10:8 (NIV) [8] We should not commit sexual immorality, as some of them did—and in one day twenty-three thousand of them died.*

God will not force us to be pure. He allows us to sin; but He judges us for our disobedience. If lightning doesn't strike when you commit your sin, don't think that means a judgment is not at hand. Do you think the people mentioned in I Corinthians chapter ten understood that if they committed sexual immorality twenty three thousand of them would die on the same day?

172

Those who do not repent, and agree with God's standard of purity, will be judged as guilty. Look at this passage in *Galatians 5:19-21 (NIV)* [19] *The acts of the sinful nature are obvious: sexual immorality, impurity and debauchery;* [20] *idolatry and witchcraft; hatred, discord, jealousy, fits of rage, selfish ambition, dissensions, factions* [21] *and envy; drunkenness, orgies, and the like. I warn you, as I did before, that those who live like this will not inherit the kingdom of God.*

You can rationalize, justify, and even ignore this passage, but it clearly states what will happen to those who do not repent of their sin of sexual immorality. They will not inherit the kingdom of God. If someone claims to be a Christian and is living in sexual immorality, they will not inherit the kingdom of God. In other words, they will not go to heaven. If a person living in sexual immorality enters heaven, then there is an error in Scripture. We need to heed the warning that Paul gave to the church of Galatia because the **Scriptures are error-free. They are never wrong.**

70% of today's young people do not see anything wrong with sex before marriage. This statistic includes young people in our churches. It would shock us to know how few make it to their wedding day as virgins. Some may rationalize that since they married the person they had premarital sex with it is okay. But the Scriptures declare that we are to keep the marriage bed pure. Any sexual activity prior to marriage is sin; even if you marry the person that you sinned with. This passage in Hebrews warns us that there will be a judgment for every act of disobedience against the marriage bed.

As the Gospel was spreading to the Gentiles, the leaders in the church of Acts got together and wrote out a list of things to abstain from. *Acts 15:29 (NIV) ²⁹ You are to abstain from food sacrificed to idols, from blood, from the meat of strangled animals and from sexual immorality. You will do well to avoid these things. Farewell.*

To abstain is an effort of self-denial. It means to walk in holiness. We must deny ourselves from the desires of the flesh and abstain from sexual immorality. Paul tells us in *I Corinthians 7:9 (NIV) ⁹ But if they cannot control themselves, they should marry, for it is better to marry than to burn with passion.* If we are having a hard time remaining pure and are of age, we should get married and not sin. Parents often urge their children to marry later in life so they can get an education. But many of these young people are having a hard time remaining pure. Paul instructs us to marry and not to burn.

3. Lust

Although the information highway has brought some good in today's world, it has also brought an element of evil. In the past, before the growth of the internet, a person had to go to seedy places to get pornography. Today, people can get pornography anywhere; in homes, on phones, and even in grocery stores. This moral decay is evident in our TV shows and commercials. Many of our current commercials would have been considered pornography 50 years ago.

Pornography has devastating effects on a generation. Since sin is progressive, its effects grow. Lust is a passion of the flesh that cannot be filled. The fire of lust grows stronger and stronger the more we feed it. Lust destroys pure mindsets and motives in relationships. It causes people to be consumed with the pleasures of self.

Jesus spoke about lust in *Matthew 5:27-30 (NIV)*
[27] "You have heard that it was said, 'Do not commit adultery.' [28] But I tell you that anyone who looks at a woman lustfully has already committed adultery with her in his heart. [29] If your right eye causes you to sin, gouge it out and throw it away. It is better for you to lose one part of your body than for your whole body to be thrown into hell. [30] And if your right hand causes you to sin, cut it off and throw it away. It is better for you to lose one part of your body than for your whole body to go into hell.

To lust is to commit adultery. The pornography rates in the church are staggering. People are hiding behind this sin because of its easy accessibility, but the effects of lust are not hidden. Marriages are being dissolved, families are being neglected, and spouses are no longer being loved and cherished. Some are even involved in pornography on levels that have become acceptable in the church. Members of the church today watch pornographic commercials, go to pornographic movies, and read pornographic material.

You may disagree. You may not watch X-rated shows, or even PG-13 rated shows; it doesn't matter. The definition of pornography is not dependent upon the ratings of society. **It is important to understand that pornography is any image depicted to arouse sexual excitement.** Our generation even uses the phrase "sex sells." Pornography is all around us. The church needs to abstain from lust by staying away from every form of this evil.

The battle to keep the marriage bed pure begins in the mind and is attained by the Spirit of Christ in us. We must not grieve the Spirit by feeding the flesh with pornographic images. The sensual media; from television shows, to commercials, to movies, to even the lyrics of songs, arouse and stimulate lust. This lust grows until people commit adultery in their hearts, or sin further and act it out with others. The church needs to turn off the pornography and stop feeding the flesh. Our children have fallen victim to the attacks of Satan because we have allowed pornography into our lives.

Lust is sexual immorality and the sexually immoral will not inherit the kingdom of God. The Bible says in *I Corinthians 6:9-11 (NIV)* [9] *Do you not know that the wicked will not inherit the kingdom of God? Do not be deceived: Neither the sexually immoral nor idolaters nor adulterers nor male prostitutes nor homosexual offenders [10] nor thieves nor the greedy nor drunkards nor slanderers nor swindlers will inherit the kingdom of God.*

We may think that we are good at hiding our sin. We may think that we have everyone fooled, but God knows and sees all. This passage reminds us that our sin will find us out. *Numbers 32:23 (NIV) [23] "But if you fail to do this, you will be sinning against the LORD; and you may be sure that your sin will find you out.* We may not get caught this time or even the next. We may not even get caught during our lifetime upon this earth. But be sure of this: One day, we will all stand before God. No one is going to get away with anything. If we have unrepentant lust; we will be guilty of adultery. If we have unrepentant premarital sex; we will be found guilty. If we have had an adulterous affair, and have not repented, we will be judged as guilty.

WAYS WE SHOULD HONOR MARRIAGE

1. Have a GREAT marriage

There is an obvious attack by Satan to discredit and destroy the family. The portrayals of dead-beat dads, incompetent parents, and people who "fall in love" with someone outside of their marriage union are common storylines today. This media onslaught against the family is working.

The church is also to blame for displaying bad marriages in the world today. Many couples in the church are dissatisfied with their marriage relationships. They have bought the lie that the grass is greener on the other side of the fence. They know that adultery and divorce are wrong, so they remain in their marriage, feeling unhappy and unfulfilled. This depiction of marriage; the depression, lack of love for one another, lack of zeal to be with their family, is devastating to society. Fathers work long hours so they can avoid time with the family. Mothers work outside the home so they can have time for themselves. Husbands and wives act as if they hardly know each other. Many couples haven't taken the time to be alone together for years. Where is the beautiful picture of how Christ loves the church? In Ephesians, Chapter 5, Paul reminds us that the love we are to have for one another is the same love that Christ has for the church. You can be assured that Christ's eyes light up when He sees His bride, the church. He is a God of love and sacrifice. He seeks to minister, please, and serve His bride to benefit her.

Where is this same kind of love in Christian marriages today? Christian marriages should display great joy, love, and unity. With Christ in us, we have the ability to love with an unconditional love. We have the ability to forgive and serve with an unconditional love.

The world should look at marriages in the church and say, "Wow! When I get married I hope that I am that happy." "I hope that my marriage makes it as long as theirs has."

For us to have great marriages, we must die to ourselves and seek to meet the other person's needs. Through this sacrifice, God will bless us and our relationships. As we put our wants aside, and meet the needs of another, we experience the power of Christ in us. When our spouse lets us down, we are able to forgive them as Christ has forgiven us. We are able to move forward in love and good deeds. The power of Christian marriages is in the mystery of Christ in us. *Ephesians 5:31-33 (NIV) [31] "For this reason a man will leave his father and mother and be united to his wife, and the two will become one flesh." [32] This is a profound mystery—but I am talking about Christ and the church. [33] However, each one of you also must love his wife as he loves himself, and the wife must respect her husband.*

Husbands fulfill your marital duty and love your wives. Meet their needs, listen to them and minister to them. Take them on dates and treat them as the queens they are. Wives respect your husbands and build them up. Encourage them; bless them; and serve them.

2. Stand up for Marriage

The media onslaught to destroy families and marriages is working. The reason it is working is because the church is not standing up and honoring the institution of marriage. If you tell a lie over and over eventually people are going to believe it. This is Satan's desire in the media onslaught.

He has told us that sex outside of marriage is not wrong through television shows, books, magazines, movies, and songs. Unfortunately, the church has participated in this evil and remained quiet. Many children who have grown up in the church have heard the lies of Satan through the media and are now acting out the immoralities that have become the "moral" norm. They commit premarital sex because they were allowed to see it depicted over and over as moral. We have not stood up to the immorality. We should have turned off the television, gotten rid of the music, and stopped seeing movies that depicted this sin as moral.
If you go to a movie and it depicts immorality as moral what should you do? Stay and watch it because you paid money to see it? Watch it, knowing it is wrong, and say nothing to your children about the evil? Or walk out as soon as an immorality is depicted as moral? You know the answer. Parents we need to teach our children to stand up for marriage.

Marriage should be honored by all and the marriage bed kept pure. The church needs to stand up for the sacred union. Instead, we watch it, listen to it, read it, buy it, and even display it in our homes. Do you own any James Bond movies? All of them depict sexual immorality as moral. Do you own any current love story movies? Most of them depict sexual immorality as moral. It shouldn't surprise us that our children are growing more and more immoral in this area.

Would you buy a book, listen to a song, or rent a movie knowing that the contents were trying to encourage you to sin? That is exactly what Satan is doing in this generation through the media.
Look at this passage in *Ephesians 5:3-7 (NIV)* *[3] But among you there must not be even a hint of sexual immorality, or of any kind of impurity, or of greed, because these are improper for God's holy people. [4] Nor should there be obscenity, foolish talk or coarse joking, which are out of place, but rather thanksgiving. [5] For of this you can be sure: No immoral, impure or greedy person–such a man is an idolater–has any inheritance in the kingdom of Christ and of God. [6] Let no one deceive you with empty words, for because of such things God's wrath comes on those who are disobedient. [7] Therefore do not be partners with them.*

Movies where unmarried people are assumed to be sleeping together is more than a hint of sexual immorality. Movies in this generation almost always include such evil. Many television shows, songs, books, and magazines have sexual immoralities in them. If you own a subscription to a magazine that has articles promoting sexual immorality, you are a partner and promoter of evil. You partner with the disobedient by supporting them. You promote the evil when people see you with the magazine or see it displayed in your home. You partner with the disobedient when you have movies in your home that depict sexual immorality as moral. You partner with the immoralities of Satan when you go to the movies that depict immorality as moral.

Stand up for the honor of marriage. Stop promoting and supporting things that dishonor the marriage bed.

3. Live pure lives

Most young people today do not understand the concept of purity. They have been warped by the liberal media. The public school system has even encouraged them with the idea of "safe sex." Consequently, the majority of young people today think nothing of having sex before marriage.

The Bible condemns any sex outside the bonds of marriage. Hebrews tells us to keep the marriage bed pure. It warns that if we don't, a judgment will be upon us. Our society encourages promiscuity. Young people are encouraged to date, go to dances, and be alone with members of the opposite sex.

Danger, danger, danger! Why encourage young people to put themselves in situations where they could sin and bring a judgment upon themselves and our nation? Our mindset needs to return to purity. We need to return to honoring the marriage bed by doing all that we can to help young people remain pure until their wedding day.

A young teenage girl does not need to open her heart to love. God created a woman to have a desire for her husband. She needs to keep that desire guarded until her wedding day. *Genesis 3:16 (NIV)*
[16] To the woman he said, "I will greatly increase your pains in childbearing; with pain you will give birth to children. **Your desire will be for your husband,** *and he will rule over you."*

The Scriptures also encourage young ladies to not awaken love until it is time. *Song of Songs 8:4 (NIV) [4] Daughters of Jerusalem, I charge you: Do not arouse or awaken love until it so desires.* We need to encourage our daughters and sons to remain pure. We need to stop encouraging them to be in situations where they could be tempted to sin. Young men need absolutely no encouragement in this area! They need their fathers and older men in the church to keep them accountable and pure.

When we send our children off to dances, we need to ask ourselves some important questions. What type of music will they be playing? Should my child be listening to "love" songs which will encourage them to be immoral? Is my child ready to be married? Do I really want to open these desires in them? The Scriptures warn us to not arouse or awaken love until its time.

What if there were three brides and you were asked to choose the purest bride for your wedding day. The first bride slept with many men. The second bride kissed and fondled many men. The third bride kept herself pure, not kissing any men or sharing her heart with anyone. She saved herself for her husband. Obviously, the third bride is the correct choice. Women need to be pure brides. Men need to be pure husbands.

Look at what Paul told young Timothy in *1 Timothy 4:12 (NIV)* *12 Don't let anyone look down on you because you are young, but set an example for the believers in speech, in life, in love, in faith and in purity.* Christian young people are to set the example in purity. Purity means to be spotless, without stain. Let's return to the true meaning of a young woman wearing white on her wedding day.

1 Thessalonians 4:1-8 (NIV) 1 Finally, brothers, we instructed you how to live in order to please God, as in fact you are living. Now we ask you and urge you in the Lord Jesus to do this more and more. 2 For you know what instructions we gave you by the authority of the Lord Jesus. 3 It is God's will that you should be sanctified: that you should avoid sexual immorality; 4 that each of you should learn to control his own body in a way that is holy and honorable, 5 not in passionate lust like the heathen, who do not know God; ^{6} and that in this matter no one should wrong his brother or take advantage of him. The Lord will punish men for all such sins, as we have already told you and warned you. ^{7} For God did not call us to be impure, but to live a holy life. ^{8} Therefore, he who rejects this instruction does not reject man but God, who gives you his Holy Spirit.

We are called to live holy lives. Paul instructs us of the kind of pure relationships we are to have until our wedding day. He leaves no clauses for girlfriends or boyfriends. I Timothy 5:1-2 (NIV) ^{1} Do not rebuke an older man harshly, but exhort him as if he were your father. Treat younger men as brothers, ^{2} older women as mothers, and younger women as sisters, with absolute purity. We are to treat one another as brothers, sisters, and mothers in the church and save ourselves for our wedding day. You would not be kissing your sister; so do not kiss another until your wedding day.

4. Repent

The greatest thing that the church can do to honor marriage is repent. We must ask God to forgive us, admit that we have sinned, and confess our sins. I John 1:9 (NIV) ^{9} If we confess our sins, he is faithful and just and will forgive us our sins and purify us from all unrighteousness.

To heal our nation, we must repent and turn from our wicked ways. 2 Chronicles 7:14 (NIV) ^{14} if my people, who are called by my name, will humble *themselves and pray and seek my face and turn from their wicked ways, then will I hear from heaven and will forgive their sin and will heal their land.*

If you are in an immoral relationship, get out of it. Get married, get away, do whatever you have to do to avoid sexual immorality. As the church, we have to stop ignoring the sin. If you know of a Christian who is living in sexual immorality, take a stand and stop associating with them. Share with them the seriousness of their sin and let them know that they will not inherit the kingdom of God unless they repent. Obey the message that Paul told the church of Corinth in *I Corinthians 5:11 (NIV) [11] But now I am writing you that you must not associate with anyone who calls himself a brother but is sexually immoral or greedy, an idolater or a slanderer, a drunkard or a swindler. With such a man do not even eat.*

Stop supporting things that dishonor marriage. Stay away from all lust and pornography. Start encouraging young people to keep the marriage bed pure. And stand up for God's standard of holiness.

When we sin sexually, we bring judgment on ourselves and our nation. We have legalized same sex unions in our nation because the church is not keeping the marriage bed pure. We are a part of the moral decline in society. God will judge us. Our nation is already experiencing the effects of these sinful lifestyle choices. If we do not repent, the decline will continue. Do we really want to continue to go down this road? We must repent!

I Corinthians 6:15-20 (NIV) ¹⁵ Do you not know that your bodies are members of Christ himself? Shall I then take the members of Christ and unite them with a prostitute? Never! ¹⁶ Do you not know that he who unites himself with a prostitute is one with her in body? For it is said, "The two will become one flesh." ¹⁷ But he who unites himself with the Lord is one with him in spirit. ¹⁸ Flee from sexual immorality. All other sins a man commits are outside his body, but he who sins sexually sins against his own body. ¹⁹ Do you not know that your body is a temple of the Holy Spirit, who is in you, whom you have received from God? You are not your own; ²⁰ you were bought at a price. Therefore honor God with your body.

We must put this sin to death. We must stop God's wrath from coming upon our nation. Look at what Paul said to the church in Colosse: *Colossians 3:5-7 (NIV) ⁵ Put to death, therefore, whatever belongs to your earthly nature: sexual immorality, impurity, lust, evil desires and greed, which is idolatry. ⁶ Because of these, the wrath of God is coming. ⁷ You used to walk in these ways, in the life you once lived.*

We may have made mistakes in the past, but it is time to look to the future. What kind of society will we be if we do not repent now? What else will be legalized? What other immoralities will be accepted in society? What other judgments will we bring upon ourselves?

The passage, in I Corinthians, Chapter 6, focused upon the danger of living sexually immoral lifestyles. Those who choose not to repent will not inherit the kingdom of God. But those who repent will be washed, sanctified, and justified because of Christ's death on the cross.

*I Corinthians 6:9-11 (NIV) ⁹ Do you not know that the wicked will not inherit the kingdom of God? Do not be deceived: Neither the sexually immoral nor idolaters nor adulterers nor male prostitutes nor homosexual offenders ¹⁰ nor thieves nor the greedy nor drunkards nor slanderers nor swindlers will inherit the kingdom of God. ¹¹ And that is what some of you were. But you were **washed**, you were **sanctified**, you were **justified** in the name of the Lord Jesus Christ and by the Spirit of our God.*

Confess your sin to God and be renewed. Repent of sinful lifestyles and let Christ begin to heal our land.

WORKSHEET FOR CHURCH GOVERNMENT
LIFE TRUTH # 7
THE CHURCH HONORS MARRIAGE

Question: How should the church view marriage?
Answer: Marriage is a sacred institution that God expects us to honor.

Hebrews 13:4 (NIV) [4] Marriage should be honored by all, and the marriage bed kept pure, for God will judge the adulterer and all the sexually immoral.

> Write out the Life Truth, question, and answer on one side of an index card and the verse on the other side. Keep it in your Bible for the week. Work on it every day individually and as a family. Have it memorized by next week.

According to Hebrews 13:4, what will happen to those who do not honor marriage?

Read Malachi 2:16. How does God feel about divorce?

There are three Scriptural reasons for dissolving a marriage. Read the passages and write the Biblical reason.
 Matthew 5:31, 32 -
 1 Corinthians 7:39 -
 1 Timothy 5:14 -
 1 Corinthians 7:12-15 -

According to Matthew 5:31-32 what does a person commit when they marry someone with an unscriptural divorce?

Read Matthew 19:3-6. Who joins a couple together in marriage? How long does God expect a couple to stay married?

Read I Corinthians 7:10-11. Who is giving this command? Sometimes there are situations when a person divorces, but not for Biblical reasons. What does this passage tell us to do in those circumstances?

According to I Timothy 5:1-2. How should young men treat older ladies? Younger ladies?

According to I Timothy 4:12. What are the five things we should be setting an example in?
S_____, L_____, L_____, F_____, P_____

How can the church do a better job of setting the example of purity in this generation?

Based on this LIFE TRUTH what can you do individually and as a family to honor marriage more? (Great resources to help raise pure children: *I Kissed Dating Goodbye* by Joshua Harris and *Before You Meet Prince Charming* by Sarah Mally)

CHURCH-GOVERNMENT LIFE TRUTH # 8 THE CHURCH IS AGAINST GAMBLING

Many things that were once recognized as sin are being accepted in today's church. The lusts of the flesh have tempted us to chase after sins that are destructive to ourselves and society.
Gambling used to be illegal in America. It was considered a vice. The word vice means: moral depravity, corruption, and wickedness. Today, this sin has been legalized by society. Church members argue that there is no scripture that says "*that thou shalt not gamble.*" The Bible is a book of morals and principles. Although it may not have a specific phrase to point out a certain evil like gambling, it does have fundamental guidelines by which God expects us to live.

No specific scripture says "*thou shalt not drive under the influence of alcohol,*" but we know God's principle is there. Driving while intoxicated is a vice in society that not only endangers the driver, but puts others in harm's way as well. Therefore, society has established laws and regulations to protect us from such an evil.

The founders of this nation understood the dangers of legalizing gambling. They recognized the consequences of such a decision. On May 26, 1777, in a circular to the brigadier-generals, General Washington wrote: *"Let vice and immorality of every kind be discouraged as much as possible in your brigade; and, as a chaplain is allowed to each regiment, see that the men regularly attend divine worship. Gaming of every kind is expressly forbidden, as being the foundation of evil, and the cause of many a brave and gallant officer's ruin."*

Our nation legalized gambling in Nevada in 1961. Since 1989, it has dramatically grown. By 2013, 23 states housed either land, riverboat, dockside, or racetrack casinos. In the 2012 American Gaming Association Report, Frank J. Fahrenkopf, Jr. stated, *"2012 national economic impact data reveals the U.S. commercial casino industry is going strong. On the strength of a third consecutive year with increased rates of growth, national gross gaming revenues for 2012 reached their second-highest level in history."* He went on to say, *"the equivalent of gross gaming revenue - rose 4.8 percent in 2012 to $37.34 billion."*

This does not include state lottery money and other forms of gambling. Mr. Fahrenkopf continued by stating, *"This year's polling not only includes an analysis of Americans' attitudes about the acceptability of casino gaming and the gambling habits and activities of casino visitors, but also an in depth look at young adult casino visitors — the very people with whom the future of our business lies."*

Gambling destroys a society by targeting our children. It blinds people of the purpose for which they were created. It consumes them with a need to fill their own selfish lusts. As stated in the American Gaming Association Report, young people are *"the very people with whom the future of our business lies."* The casino industry has a legal age limit of 21. The highest percentage of the people who visited last year were between the ages of 21-35. Casinos boast that one third of the American population visit their establishments. They had 76.1 million visitors in 2012. Only 23 states have legalized casinos, so a very high percentage of the people living near a casino are gambling.

Twenty-three states brought in $37.34 billion dollars through casino gambling in 2012. NBC news reported in an article titled, *"Powerball Profits Don't All Go Where You Think They Do"*, that state-run lotteries across 44 states brought in nearly $69 billion dollars in 2012. This means $106.34 billion dollars was gambled in 2012. This doesn't even include every type of gambling. There is also gambling with sporting events, raffle tickets, bingo, etc.

What defines gambling? Gambling is playing a game for money or property. It is betting on a chance outcome. It is risking something that you have in an attempt to win more.

"*It's just for fun!*" people exclaim. Others say that it's their own money. If they want to gamble a certain amount, how can that be wrong? It is wrong because they are justifying sin. I know a lady whose Senior

193

Center picks people up once a week and takes them to the casino. She was taught as a child that gambling was a sin, but decided to go and enjoyed it. She described herself to me as a "responsible" gambler. She informed me that every week she only took $20 dollars and when that was gone she was done. This justification to sin is prevalent in the church today. Many people think that if they pay their bills, it is okay for them to gamble part of their money. After all, they could win big one day.

It is hard to distinguish truth from lies when it comes to gambling in our nation. Many claim that a lot of the money goes into the school systems to help with education. The reality is that no more than eleven cents on the dollar goes to help schools and other community projects; a small percentage of the billions of dollars generated each year in the gambling industry.

Even if schools received most of the money, would that justify gambling? No! Does the end justify the means? No! The argument that a certain percentage is given to the schools should not be the issue. The issue is whether or not it is justified according to God's Word.

Gambling, by its very definition, is what the Bible calls greed or covetousness. To gamble is to invest something that you own in the hopes of gaining more. People invest money to win games at casinos, participate in raffles, and buy lottery tickets in the hopes of winning something more. Churches are guilty of this form of gambling, too. Whenever you spend money to win money and/or property, with no work being done, you are gambling.

HERE ARE SEVEN BIBLICAL REASONS AGAINST GAMBLING

1. Gambling destroys our work ethic

In our Self-Government Life Truth #10, we learned that we are to provide for our daily necessities; we are to provide for our families; we are to provide for those in need. *Titus 3:14 (NIV) [14] Our people must learn to **devote themselves to doing what is good, in order that they may provide for daily necessities and not live unproductive lives.***

An unproductive life is a life that does not work and does not earn the bread they eat. *2 Thessalonians 3:11-12 (NIV) [11] We hear that some among you are idle. They are not busy; they are busybodies. [12] Such people we command and urge in the Lord Jesus Christ to settle down and **earn the bread they eat.***

Winnings are not earning the bread that you eat. It is not the morally responsible way to live our lives. We are to live self-controlled lives that are free from the love of money. Hard work brings profit. This is the role that God has called us to. Societies crumble when they allow "get rich quick" schemes to grow and become acceptable. These schemes destroy. They do not build up a society.

Proverbs 14:23 (NIV) [23] All hard work brings a profit, but mere talk leads only to poverty.

Acts 20:35 (NIV) [35] In everything I did, I showed you that by this kind of hard work we must help the weak, remembering the words the Lord Jesus himself said: 'It is more blessed to give than to receive.'"

Our sinful flesh wants to be lazy. We want to have everything given to us. But Christ wants us to be pillars of society. We are to not only provide for our needs, but we are to provide for the needs of others in society.

Scriptures warn us against the "get rich quick" ideas and false dreams. *Proverbs 28:19-20 (NIV) [19] He who works his land will have abundant food, but the one who chases fantasies will have his fill of poverty. [20] A faithful man will be richly blessed, but one eager to get rich will not go unpunished.*

Gambling destroys the work ethic of a society. It also increases bankruptcy filings. Professor John Warren Kindt calculated that for every dollar in gambling revenue that a state takes in, it costs taxpayers $1.90. Society pays for lost wages, counseling centers, welfare costs for destroyed families, and the increases in criminal behaviors as people seek ways to pay off their debts.

Gambling takes people away from the hard work that needs to be invested in a strong society. Gamblers become lazy; trying to win big and retire. Gambling does not create wealth. It only redistributes wealth to others. Casinos claim that they are creating jobs and bringing tax revenue into society, but that is not the case. People are losing money, lives are being destroyed, and taxes are continuing to rise as we deal with the effects of this sin.

It is hard work that produces money and goods for society. Gambling produces neither. Gambling takes what others have; making very few rich.

2. Gambling is not loving my neighbor

The definition of greed is an eager desire to gain more. Greed is closely tied to coveting which is the desire to have what others own. When a person gambles, they are hoping to gain what others own. People get together to bet their money; coveting to win everyone else's money. Greed and coveting are both condemned in Scripture. They are not the reflection of a Christ-like attitude.

People bet on the lottery. They hope to win the jackpot. What is the jackpot? It is a culmination of everyone's money. When you buy a lottery ticket, you are coveting everyone else's money. You desire what they own. This is the very definition of coveting.

The church should abstain from and stand up against every type of gambling. It is a terrible vice that leads people into sin and selfishness. Our two greatest commands are to love God and to love others.

Romans 13:8-10 (NIV) ⁸ Let no debt remain outstanding, except the continuing debt to love one another, for he who loves his fellowman has fulfilled the law. ⁹ The commandments, "Do not commit adultery," "Do not murder," "Do not steal," "Do not covet," and whatever other commandment there may be, are summed up in this one rule: "Love your neighbor as yourself." ¹⁰ Love does no harm to its neighbor. Therefore love is the fulfillment of the law. When you gamble, you are not loving your brother, you are desiring to take from your brother.

Christian love is sacrificial. It involves giving to others. *I John 3:16-18 (NIV) ¹⁶ This is how we know what love is: Jesus Christ laid down his life for us. And we ought to lay down our lives for our brothers. ¹⁷ If anyone has material possessions and sees his brother in need but has no pity on him, how can the love of God be in him? ¹⁸ Dear children, let us not love with words or tongue but with actions and in truth.*

When people gamble, they are not hoping that the other people get their money. They are hoping that they take other people's money. They are hoping that others lose and they win. Jesus told us in *Matthew 7:12 (NIV) ¹² So in everything, do to others what you would have them do to you, for this sums up the Law and the Prophets.*

How can you assure people that you will not take their money just as you do not want them to take your money? You do not gamble! That is how you can make sure you are treating your brothers as you would want to be treated. A characteristic of love in 1 Corinthians, Chapter 13, is that it is not self-seeking. Christian love considers others better than themselves. It seeks to do others good and not harm.

3. Gambling is a root to all kinds of evil

The root of gambling is to gain more. People claim that it is just a game for entertainment. But the entertainment they are seeking is the rush that they get when they win.

Society needs to be built upon godly virtues like self-control, self-restraint, patience, and contentment. Legalizing gambling opened the door to many vices that we are facing today. We live in an impatient world. The Scriptures tell us about the evils of greed. *1 Timothy 6:10 (NIV)* [10] *For the love of money is a root of all kinds of evil. Some people, eager for money, have wandered from the faith and pierced themselves with many griefs.*

The Bible warns us about these foolish and harmful desires that plunge us into ruin and destruction. It is a proven fact that gambling destroys families. People

become secretive. People neglect their spouses and their children. People lose their family's income and security. Many even steal from their own families and others to support their addiction.
Gambling opens the door to all kinds of evil. Prostitution and other sexual immoralities occur more in areas of gambling. Nevada has the highest suicide rate in the nation, as well as over 130 pages of advertisements relating to prostitution in their yellow pages. Crime also increases as gamblers become desperate and distraught.

Christians should know better because the Word of God states, *"the love of money is a root of all kinds of evil."*

4. Gambling is a bad witness

Are you satisfied with God? Are you satisfied with what the Lord has provided for you? The Bible tells us to be satisfied with what the Lord has provided for us. This teaching is about being content with what you have. Today many people are dissatisfied with their lives. People believe the lie that money will make everything better. This lie has even come into the church. Many believers are eager for money and are gambling to get rich. They may not go to the casinos, but they are playing the lotteries, hoping money will solve their problems as well as indulge their flesh with materialism.

Money is not the answer to all of life's issues. Jesus is the answer to all of life's issues. When we believe that money will solve all of our problems, we have just made money an idol. We are commanded as Christians to put to death this kind of idolatry.

Colossians 3:5 (NIV) [5] Put to death, therefore, whatever belongs to your earthly nature: sexual immorality, impurity, lust, evil desires and greed, which is idolatry. If you love money, you will never have enough money. *Ecclesiastes 5:10 (NIV) [10] Whoever loves money never has money enough; whoever loves wealth is never satisfied with his income. This too is meaningless.*

John the Baptist came on the scene to prepare the way for the Lord. One of the sins that he addressed was contentment. He told the people that they needed to repent and be content with what the Lord had provided for them. Be so content with what you have, that if you have two of something, share one with someone in need. Don't be so self-focused that all you care about is acquiring more.

Luke 3:9-14 (NIV) [9] The ax is already at the root of the trees, and every tree that does not produce good fruit will be cut down and thrown into the fire." [10] "What should we do then?" the crowd asked. [11] John answered, "The man with two tunics should share with him who has none, and the one who has food should do the same." [12] Tax collectors also came to be baptized. "Teacher," they asked, "what should we do?" [13] "Don't collect any more than you are required to," he told them. [14] Then some soldiers asked him, "And what should we do?" He replied, "Don't extort money and don't accuse people falsely—be content with your pay."

He told them to be content; to be satisfied with what the Lord has provided. Be content with your pay. Don't start looking for ungodly ways to earn more money whether it be through extortion or gambling. Be godly in your character and produce good fruit. Paul understood this teaching and he told us to do the same in *Philippians 4:11-13 (NIV) [11] I am not saying this because I am in need, for I have learned to be content whatever the circumstances. [12] I know what it is to be in need, and I know what it is to have plenty. I have learned the secret of being content in any and every situation, whether well fed or hungry, whether living in plenty or in want. [13] I can do everything through him who gives me strength.*

Paul learned to be content whether well fed or hungry. Paul was satisfied with Jesus and the relationship that he had with Him no matter what the circumstances. Are you satisfied with your life as it is? Do you desire more things and more money for your satisfaction? The church should be satisfied with Jesus and ready to meet Him every day. Are you ready to meet Jesus today?

The church should be an example of contentment to the world. After all, this place is not our home. We should not be consumed with acquiring more. In fact, Jesus condemns those who desire to build bigger and bigger barns to store "their" stuff. We are called to higher purposes as Christians. As Jesus said in *Acts 20:35 (NIV) ³⁵ In everything I did, I showed you that by this kind of hard work we must help the weak, remembering the words the Lord Jesus himself said: 'It is more blessed to give than to receive.'"*

The church needs to recognize man's sinful nature and strive to keep his earthly passions under control. Opening doors that arouse these passions only leads to destruction. Greed is a passion that is within us all. We need to be denying the passions of the flesh. Jesus said in *Mark 7:21-23 (NIV) ²¹ For from within, out of men's hearts, come evil thoughts, sexual immorality, theft, murder, adultery, ²² greed, malice, deceit, lewdness, envy, slander, arrogance and folly. ²³ All these evils come from inside and make a man 'unclean.'"*

Sin is a dangerous thing. It brings ruin and destruction. Many young people are being ensnared into the passions of the flesh through gambling. Paul warns us to be content and to stay away from the desire to get rich. *I Timothy 6:6-9 (NIV) ⁶ But godliness with contentment is great gain. ⁷ For we brought nothing into the world, and we can take nothing out of it. ⁸ But if we have food and clothing, we will be content with that. ⁹ People who want to get rich fall into temptation and a trap and into many foolish and harmful desires that plunge men into ruin and destruction.*

The church needs to be teaching people to stay free from the love of money. It is a bad witness to gamble. Gambling shows a lack of contentment with God and all that He has provided. *Hebrews 13:5 (NIV) [5] Keep your lives free from the love of money and be content with what you have, because God has said, "Never will I leave you; never will I forsake you."*

When we gamble, even if it is just a "little" money, we are being accomplices to someone's demise. Perhaps the person we are gambling with is an addict who is destroying his family. Perhaps the person we are playing with will become addicted and destroy their life. Don't be guilty of causing someone to stumble because of something you have approved of in your life.

Even a "little" sin manages to destroy many lives. The church is not to approve of sinful addictions. Our examples should lead others to follow Christ; not follow paths that lead them into destruction. So even if you only play for a "little" money, it is a sin and a bad example for others.

5. Gambling is bad stewardship

We are stewards and not owners. It is our responsibility as stewards to handle the money that God provides us with very carefully. The lure and lies of gambling are devastating to society. The flesh desires to be wealthy. The media promotes the few who actually win the lottery as stars and lifts them up as examples for us to follow.

Satan feeds the greed within our hearts and fills our hearts with lies. He wants people to believe that it's only a few dollars. He wants people to think they might be a big winner someday. But the reality of gambling is this: Most people do not win. Most people are losers in the game of chance. Most people squander away the provisions that God gives them for their needs and the needs of those around them. When we stand before God, we will be held accountable, as stewards, as to how we have handled His wealth. Do we really want to stand before Him and tell him that we have gambled away a lot of His money in the hopes of winning more; when He has clearly told us to keep our lives free from the love of money?

Gambling is corrupt and invades society, placing a chokehold on a nation. Many politicians today are funded through the revenues of gambling. If gambling were good for the economy, we'd have a lot of rich gamblers. Instead, we have very few winners and many, many losers. The people who are becoming wealthy off of gambling are the owners and politicians. *Proverbs 22:16 (NIV) 16 He who oppresses the poor to increase his wealth and he who gives gifts to the rich—both come to poverty.*

Have we forgotten that the Lord is the one who will bless our economy? *Deuteronomy 8:17-18 (NIV) 17 You may say to yourself, "My power and the strength of my hands have produced this wealth for me." 18 But remember the LORD your God, for it is he who gives you the ability to produce wealth, and so confirms his covenant, which he swore to your forefathers, as it is today.*

God is the giver of wealth. We are to acquire it through honesty, integrity, hard work, self-control, and responsibility. One day we will give an account for how we handled **His wealth**.

Look at what Jesus said about being a good steward of His money in *Luke 16:11-13 (NIV)* *¹¹ So if you have not been trustworthy in handling worldly wealth, who will trust you with true riches? ¹² And if you have not been trustworthy with someone else's property, who will give you property of your own? ¹³ "No servant can serve two masters. Either he will hate the one and love the other, or he will be devoted to the one and despise the other. You cannot serve both God and money."*

6. Gambling violates the poor

Many people who gamble cannot afford to gamble. While all money should be used for good purposes, many people are spending what should be going to pay bills and other expenses on the lottery. It is a proven fact that the majority of the people who gamble are the poor. They are placing their hope in the "god" of money. The hope of many is to become rich.

There is a special place in God's heart for the poor and the needy. Those that win lotteries (like the

Powerball) are taking a lot of poor people's money. Do you really want to get rich at the expense of the poor's misfortune? We can justify it and say that they didn't have to play or they made their own choice to gamble. But the Scriptures are clear that we should not be taking from the poor. Instead, we are commanded to help the poor. *Proverbs 14:31 (NIV) [31] He who oppresses the poor shows contempt for their Maker, but whoever is kind to the needy honors God.* We should be seeking to educate the poor in the ways of God. We need to be an example of godly living for them. God commands us to help the poor and be open-handed towards them. This is part of the process of having a healthy society. Many times we want to hide the poor, blame them for all of their misfortunes, and lend no helping hands.

Proverbs 19:17 (NIV) [17] He who is kind to the poor lends to the LORD, and he will reward him for what he has done.

If we cared about the poor, we would cry out for justice for them. We would seek to stop the ungodly practice of gambling. *Proverbs 29:7 (NIV) [7] The righteous care about justice for the poor, but the wicked have no such concern.* If we really care about our brothers, we will stop welcoming these vices in society and urge others to do the same.

7. Gambling is sin

Gambling is greed and covetousness and both are condemned in the Word of God. To justify gambling in any form is to go against the Word of God. All gambling is sin. From raffles that are for "good causes" to bingo, to small bets in people's homes. If the raffle is for a good cause, just give the money. Do not seek to gain more through your bet. It is improper for us to want what others have for the benefit of ourselves. To want what others have, so that we can have more, is coveting. It is sinful. On the Day of Judgment, we are not going to be judged by how much we have; we will be judged by who we are.

It is sad when more and more Christians are interested in *winning* the lottery than *winning* lost souls. *Proverbs 11:30 (NIV)* [30] *The fruit of the righteous is a tree of life, and he who wins souls is wise.* It used to be that Christians would have been ashamed to go to a public place to gamble. George Washington would have been ashamed to go into a convenience store and buy a lottery ticket, but he was not afraid to share his belief in Jesus as Lord. Today, the opposite is true. Many Christians gamble publicly, but are ashamed to share Christ publicly. They are ashamed to share their faith with others, but they are not ashamed to buy lottery tickets or go to a casino. We need to return to the desire for godly winnings of lost souls and turn away from the desire of worldly winnings.

Proverbs 11:4 (NIV) *⁴ Wealth is worthless in the day of wrath, but righteousness delivers from death.*

The church needs to be against all forms of gambling. We need to be teaching against the destructive evils that it brings into a society. We opened the door to gambling in the 1960's and are now experiencing the evils that came with it. We must abstain from our sinful desires and seek to walk in righteousness. If our generation continues to legalize more and more sin, we will continue to pay the consequences.

When we know people who are buying lottery tickets, we need to speak up and tell them that money is not the answer to life's problems. Jesus is the answer and gambling is sin. Look at this passage in *Ephesians 5:3-7 (NIV)* *³ But among you there must not be even a hint of sexual immorality, or of any kind of impurity, or of greed, because these are improper for God's holy people. ⁴ Nor should there be obscenity, foolish talk or coarse joking, which are out of place, but rather thanksgiving. ⁵ For of this you can be sure: No immoral, impure or greedy person—such a man is an idolater—has any inheritance in the kingdom of Christ and of God. ⁶ Let no one deceive you with empty words, for because of such things God's wrath comes on those who are disobedient. ⁷ Therefore do not be partners with them.*

We are not to be partners with the disobedient. Gambling is partnering with them. We need to stay away from such vices in society. We need to speak up for Biblical principles. The next time you desire to buy a lottery ticket in the hopes that you can gain more, remember that gambling is sin. We should not be a part of the downfall of our society. We should be leading our society in Christian character and in Christian love for one another.

WORKSHEET FOR CHURCH GOVERNMENT LIFE TRUTH # 8
THE CHURCH IS AGAINST GAMBLING

Question: How should the church view gambling?
Answer: Gambling is the sin of greed and there should not be even a hint of greed in a Christian's life.

Ephesians 5:3 (NIV) ³ But among you there must not be even a hint of sexual immorality, or of any kind of impurity, or of greed, because these are improper for God's holy people.

> Write out the Life Truth, question, and answer on one side of an index card and the verse on the other side. Keep it in your Bible for the week. Work on it every day individually and as a family. Have it memorized by next week.

Read Ephesians 5:3-7. In verse 3, what three things are Christian's not to even have a hint of in their lives?

Can a greedy person enter into the kingdom of Christ? (v 5)

Read Colossians 3:5. What does the Bible call greed? Greed is an eager desire to gain more. What does Proverbs 28:20 tell us about a greedy person?

Read Exodus 20:17. To covet is to want something that someone else has. Explain how gambling is coveting?

Coveting is a sin. Being greedy is a sin. Gambling is coveting and being greedy, so is gambling a sin? Explain.

Read Philippians 4:10-13. Paul learned to be content (satisfied) with what God provided for him. What do you think the secret is to being content in all circumstances?

Read Acts 16:22-25. What was Paul doing in this tough circumstance?   How can this help someone be content?

Read 1 Timothy 6:6-10. What did we bring into the world?   What will we take out of this world?   How should this truth effect the way we live?

Verse 9 - What kinds of traps do people fall into?

Verse 9 - Circle the correct statement:

The love of money is a root of all kinds of evil.
Money is the root of all kinds of evil.

Why is it important to know the difference between these two statements?

Based on this LIFE TRUTH what can you do individually and as a family to avoid the traps of loving money? How can you help others understand that gambling is a sin?

CHURCH-GOVERNMENT LIFE TRUTH # 9
THE CHURCH SUFFERS FOR CHRIST

You've probably heard it said, *"If God is a God of love then why does He allow good people to suffer?"* Most likely you've even wrestled with this question at some point in your own life. There is suffering all around us. But why? Does it have a purpose? Is there an explanation for it? People have questioned this issue since creation.

Natural causes of suffering are a result of Adam and Eve eating the forbidden fruit. When they ate the fruit, sin was brought into the world. Sin brought decay, destruction, and death. Natural disasters, like tornados, earthquakes, tsunamis, and hurricanes, are tragedies where many innocent people suffer. Malicious evil is another cause of suffering. This suffering results from a deliberate decision to perform some type of malicious act. Finally, there are accidents and mistakes that cause unintentional suffering.

Even though we can decipher the causes, it still doesn't help us understand the reasons why God allows suffering. God is all powerful. When a hurricane heads for land, why doesn't God stop it or have it head in a different direction? Why does God allow the hurricane to hit land and cause suffering?

Why does God allow other types of accidental suffering? Why doesn't He stop malicious suffering? Scriptures do help us to better understand the *whys* of suffering. As we study the Bible, we begin to see God's purposes more clearly. But this side of heaven, we may never fully understand the reasons why God allows certain types of suffering.

One sobering fact about suffering is that most of the suffering we endure is man's own fault. Adam and Eve allowed sin to enter into this world; not God. God created us with a free will. We suffer when we do not choose righteousness. In fact, Satan was not created to cause evil. He was created to glorify God. But Satan chose to turn away from God. He is still influencing people today to commit sins that bring evil and suffering.

Some Christians believe that once you are saved, you should be exempt from all forms of suffering. The truth is that no one is exempt from suffering until they get to heaven. In this sinful world, everyone will suffer. Jesus said in *John 16:33 (NIV)* [33] "*I have told you these things, so that in me you may have peace.* **In this world you will have trouble**. *But take heart! I have overcome the world.*" The word trouble can also be translated tribulation or suffering. Not only are we told in the Scriptures that we will suffer, but the Bible tells Christians that they are called to suffer for Christ.

The most important part of understanding the *why* is that we can trust God. When we cannot understand or comprehend a specific type of suffering, we can trust that God has a plan. He has a reason. He is always in control.

Here are some Biblical points about suffering:

1. No one is excluded from suffering

Some believe that if you do everything right you should never have to suffer. We would have to ignore some very important Scriptures to make this a true statement. Obedience equals blessings. Through obedience, we do save ourselves from many hardships and sufferings. But there is no guarantee in God's Word that we will not suffer.

The book of Job is a good example of this doctrine. The book begins by telling us that Job was a righteous man. *Job 1:1 (NIV)* [1] *In the land of Uz there lived a man whose name was Job.* **This man was blameless and upright; he feared God and shunned evil.**
If Job was a righteous man, and obedience equals blessings, then he should never have experienced sufferings, right? While obedience does equal blessings, God has a higher plan in allowing some types of suffering. The book of Job reveals to us that God brought Job to Satan so he could tempt him and test his faith. Satan was sure that Job would turn away from God when God did not bless him.

God allowed Job to go through a lot of painful suffering to test his faith. Do you love God enough to continue to praise Him and serve Him through your suffering? Will you endure like Job? It says in *Job 13:15 (NIV)* *¹⁵ Though he slay me, yet will I hope in him.*

The Bible tells us in the New Testament that some men from Galilee came to Jerusalem to offer sacrifices and Pilate had them killed. We do not know the details but we do know that the people were upset about this injustice and the fact that God allowed them to suffer in this way. The passage states in *Luke 13:1-5 (NIV)* *¹ Now there were some present at that time who told Jesus about the Galileans whose blood Pilate had mixed with their sacrifices. ² Jesus answered, "Do you think that these Galileans were worse sinners than all the other Galileans because they suffered this way? ³ I tell you, no! But unless you repent, you too will all perish. ⁴ Or those eighteen who died when the tower in Siloam fell on them—do you think they were more guilty than all the others living in Jerusalem? ⁵ I tell you, no! But unless you repent, you too will all perish."*

Jesus is revealing that no one is exempt from suffering. When we sin against God, we deserve the death penalty. The Galileans who suffered unjustly were as guilty as any of the other Galileans, because all have sinned and fallen short of the glory of God. (Romans 3:23)

We are all guilty before God and deserve death and hell for the consequences of our sin. Our only hope is exactly what Jesus said twice in this passage, *"But unless you repent, you too will all perish."* We must repent, trust in what Jesus did for us on the cross, and make Him our Lord, in order to be free from eternal suffering.

Once we repent and begin to follow Christ, it still doesn't mean that we will be free from suffering. We may even have a tower fall on us like the tower of Siloam. We all are sinners before God and our sin brings consequences. It brings death and suffering whether we have sinned a little or a lot. Look at what James says in *James 2:10 (NIV)* [10] *For whoever keeps the whole law and yet stumbles at just one point **is guilty of breaking all of it**.*

The question we began with was, *"If God is a God of love then why does He allow good people to suffer?"* Jesus said in *Mark 10:18 (NIV)* [18] *"Why do you call me good?" Jesus answered. **"No one is good--except God alone.*** We are all sinners and in need of God's grace.

2. God expects us to handle suffering well

Job exclaimed in his suffering, *"Though he slay me, yet will I hope in him."* Today many people need God to fix things in their lives (like their health, relationships, or finances) before they are ready to praise Him. They expect God to change their circumstances before they'll put their trust in Him.

God is more concerned with our character than He is our comforts. Comfort often turns into idolatry which only separates us from Him. God desires for us to love Him more than anything; more than our circumstances, more than our relationships, more than our finances, and more than our health.

The Bible says in *I Thessalonians 5:16-18 (NIV) ¹⁶ Be joyful always; ¹⁷ pray continually; ¹⁸ give thanks in all circumstances, for this is God's will for you in Christ Jesus.* God's will is for us to be thankful in our suffering. Why? It is by being thankful during suffering that we can be a powerful witness to those around us. If this life is our only hope, then suffering through it would be meaningless. This world expects those who are suffering to be complainers, depressed, ungrateful, and unhappy. So when Christians are thankful during their suffering, it makes people take notice.

If I was paralyzed, but had an attitude of hope, praise, and thankfulness, my actions would give God the glory. I would also have a powerful testimony about my future hope of heaven. I might be missing out on the skiing, running, and other activities on this earth, but certainly not for all eternity. In fact, my future home would be in a place with no suffering at all. Thankfulness during suffering is possible when you have your focus on heaven and not on this earth. This kind of living is a powerful witness to the world. Job said it this way in *Job 17:13-15 (NIV) ¹³ If the only home I hope for is the grave, if I spread out my bed in darkness, [14] if I say to corruption, 'You are my father,' and to the worm, 'My mother' or 'My sister,' [15] where then is my hope? Who can see any hope for me?* Christians, we have a great hope! One day, we will be removed from this world of suffering.

Another powerful way to help people understand about the suffering we experience in this life, is when Christians sacrifice their own wants in order to help others who are suffering. Jesus said that when one person is suffering; everyone is suffering. We should be living for opportunities to help others who are suffering, instead of living for our own pleasures. If you've been blessed with the luxuries of this world, use them to bless others, not just yourself and your family. Minister to others who are less fortunate than you. Use your resources to bless those around you.

If you have so many luxuries that you do not have time to attend church, help others, or are in financial bondage to them, you need to repent. When people see Christians sacrificing their money, time, and possessions to bless others, it causes them to rethink their positions on life. It causes people to question why someone would reach out to help another when they could choose to spend the time or money on themselves.

We are to be the light of the world who point people toward heaven. These earthly things do not mean a thing in light of eternity. We must have a great attitude whether we are the one suffering or someone else is suffering. We can have this great attitude as long as we keep our eyes on Jesus and our goal of heaven!

God allows suffering for specific reasons

1. Salvation

There are examples in Scripture when God comes to the rescue of those who are suffering. When God intervenes and saves them from their suffering, they accept Him and praise Him. The Bible says in, *Luke 13:10-13 (NIV) [10] On a Sabbath Jesus was teaching in one of the synagogues, [11] and a woman was there who had been crippled by a spirit for eighteen years. She was bent over and could not straighten up at all. [12] When Jesus saw her, he called her forward and said to her, "Woman, you are set free from your infirmity." [13] Then he put his hands on her, and immediately she straightened up and praised God.*

Her healing caused her to praise God. When God delivered her, it brought forth praise to Him. How do you think she praised God? Do you think that she gave him a half-hearted thanks? Or do you think that she jumped, shouted, and told everyone that she saw what God had done for her? The Bible says that she suffered with that crippled spirit for 18 years. What if she had only suffered a few minutes and then Jesus healed her? Do you think her praise would have been as passionate?

I'm sure she was glad that she went to the synagogue that day. Every week, Christians need to be filling our churches, hoping that their day of healing has come. Can God still heal? Yes! Perhaps, your suffering is almost over. Are you having a good attitude? Have you learned to be content (satisfied) even in your suffering? Can you praise Jesus and be thankful that you are suffering?

Another healing is recorded in the Gospel of John. *John 4:46-53 (NIV) 46 Once more he visited Cana in Galilee, where he had turned the water into wine. And there was a certain royal official whose son lay sick at Capernaum. 47 When this man heard that Jesus had arrived in Galilee from Judea, he went to him and begged him to come and heal his son, who was close to death. 48 "Unless you people see miraculous signs and wonders," Jesus told him, "you will never believe." 49 The royal official said, "Sir, come down before my child dies." 50 Jesus replied, "You may go. Your son will live." The man took Jesus at his word and departed. 51 While he was still on the way, his servants met him with the news that his boy was living. 52 When he inquired as to the time when his son got better, they said to him, "The fever left him yesterday at the seventh hour." 53 Then the father realized that this was the exact time at which Jesus had said to him, "Your son will live." So he and all his household believed.*

This royal official came to Jesus for the healing of his son. There is a high likelihood that this official may never have come to Christ except through the suffering of his son. It was the suffering of his son that caused him to seek Jesus. Jesus even acknowledges the fact that we are often so hard-headed that we need to see miraculous signs and wonders to believe. He acknowledges in another passage that even though we see the miraculous signs, we still may not believe.

Salvation came to this official because his son was suffering. The Bible says that when he realized that Jesus healed his son, he believed. Not only did he believe, but his entire household was saved through the suffering of his son.

The son must have been suffering greatly for the man to pursue Jesus. If the official had believed that his son would get better on his own, do you think he would have been as passionate about insisting that Jesus come and heal him? No. Was the suffering of the son worth it when the entire household got saved? Yes! Sometimes it takes suffering to wake us up to the fact that we need Jesus in this sinful world.

Sanctification

Sanctification is the process of being made holy. Jesus speaks about sanctification in John, Chapter 15, when he talks about a gardener pruning a tree. Sometimes things need to be cut off of us that are dead and draining us of the life that God longs for us. God's desire is for us to be conformed into the image of

Christ. He longs for our character to be changed and for us to spend an eternity with Him in heaven.

There are other lessons, besides the need for a good attitude, that can be learned through different types of suffering. Paul spoke to the church in Antioch in Acts 14:22 (NIV) *[22] strengthening the disciples and encouraging them to remain true to the faith. "We must go through many hardships to enter the kingdom of God," they said.* We must go through many hardships? Paul had to endure a spiritual torment that God said He would not remove. Thankfully, God gave Paul a reason for the torment. *2 Corinthians 12:7 (NIV) [7] To keep me from becoming conceited because of these surpassingly great revelations, there was given me a thorn in my flesh, a messenger of Satan, to torment me.*

The suffering of Paul had a specific purpose. The Scriptures declare that God will not share His glory with another and that God hates pride. If Paul would have become conceited, then he would not have been allowed into heaven. The most loving thing that God could do for Paul was to allow him to have that spirit to torment him. It is hard to grasp this truth, unless we focus on the goal of heaven.

God prunes us for our benefit. He wants us to be fruitful for Him and to be in His presence forever. God may not reveal the *whys* of our suffering, but we can always trust Him, His plan, and His purpose for our lives.

2. To discipline us

Suffering for discipline is different than suffering for sanctification. When we sin, God disciplines us. It is because we have either gone astray or we are doing something that is wrong. We experience the effects of our sin and the suffering that comes with it. But there are other times when God uses natural causes to bring on suffering in the hopes of getting our attention. In both cases, He corrects us out of love, just as loving parents do when they discipline their own children. The only way to lessen the severity of our suffering is by obeying God's Word.

Hebrews 12:5-6 (NIV) ⁵ And you have forgotten that word of encouragement that addresses you as sons: "My son, do not make light of the Lord's discipline, and do not lose heart when he rebukes you, ⁶ because the Lord disciplines those he loves, and he punishes everyone he accepts as a son."

A famous passage in the Old Testament tells about God's people repenting of their sins and how God restored their land. *2 Chronicles 7:13-15 (NIV) ¹³ "When I shut up the heavens so that there is no rain, or command locusts to devour the land or send a plague among my people, ¹⁴ if my people, who are called by my name, will humble themselves and pray and seek my face and turn from their wicked ways, then will I hear from heaven and will forgive their sin and will heal their land. ¹⁵ Now my eyes will be open and my ears attentive to the prayers offered in this place.*

Many times we forget verse 13, which explains how God allowed suffering to awaken His people to repentance. God wants to intervene for us. The wind and the waves obey Him when He speaks. He can calm a storm just like He did for the disciples. But the disciples had to ask God to intervene, and so do we.

We should be glad that God allows us to suffer and go through discipline because it means that He loves us and cares for us. If the official's son had not gotten sick, the entire family would not have been saved. If Paul had not been given a spirit to torment him, he would not have been saved. If God didn't allow us to go through suffering, we would not grow and seek to become more like Him. The Psalmist wrote in *Psalm 119:67 (NIV)* [67] *Before I was afflicted I went astray, but now I obey your word. Psalm 119:71 (NIV)* [71] *It was good for me to be afflicted so that I might learn your decrees.*

I have personally been through painful suffering that has changed my character. Being refined in the fire hurts, but the benefits are worth it. I praise God for the work that's He's doing in me. Suffering can be very productive if we handle it with the right attitude. Paul could have demanded that God remove the spirit that tormented him. He could have turned away from Christ and refused to build God's kingdom. But he didn't. In fact, the phrase *"give thanks in all circumstances"* was penned by Paul.

3. For persecutions

What if you were a sports fanatic, got dressed up in your team's paraphernalia, and went to a game? If you went to the stadium of your team, you would be accepted. But if you went into the stadium of another team, most likely you would get some stares and a few choice comments about your attire. You would expect to get some persecution and experience a little suffering by the other fans. So why not expect persecution and suffering on this earth, since you are in the opposing teams territory?

Ephesians 6:12 (NIV) [12] For our struggle is not against flesh and blood, but against the rulers, against the authorities, against the powers of this dark world and against the spiritual forces of evil in the heavenly realms. Satan is the prince of this world and God has given him the ability to attack. We are in the enemy's territory and because of that, we will experience sufferings.

When we become born again, we put on the character of Christ. This clothing is like putting on the opposing team's attire. We are making a bold statement in our character that we no longer support the old team. In fact, Paul says this in *Romans 12:2 (NIV) [2] Do not conform any longer to the pattern of this world, but be transformed by the renewing of your mind.* As Christians, we are leaving the rules, regulations, and philosophies of this world, and we are embracing the teachings of Christ. *Ephesians 2:1-3 (NIV) [1] As for you, you were dead in your transgressions and sins, ² in which you used to live when you followed the ways of this world and of the ruler of the kingdom of the air, the spirit who is now at work in those who are disobedient. ³ All of us also lived among them at one time, gratifying the cravings of our sinful nature and following its desires and thoughts. Like the rest, we were by nature objects of wrath.*

We were objects of wrath (suffering) but in Christ we have been redeemed. Eventually, we will be free from all suffering. But as long as we live in this world, there will be suffering.

Being a Christian means that the opposing side is going to persecute you. Paul said it this way in *Philippians 1:29 (NIV) ²⁹ For it has been granted to you on behalf of Christ not only to believe on him, but also to suffer for him.* The opposing team may do more than just say a few mean words to you. Look at this passage in *Acts 5:40-41 (NIV) ⁴⁰ His speech persuaded them. They called the apostles in and had them flogged. Then they ordered them not to speak in the name of Jesus, and let them go.* ⁴¹ **The apostles left the Sanhedrin, rejoicing because they had been counted worthy of suffering disgrace for the Name.**

2 Timothy 3:12 (NIV) ¹² In fact, everyone who wants to live a godly life in Christ Jesus will be persecuted,

Paul wrote many of the books in the New Testament. He went on missionary journeys and started churches for God's kingdom. Paul had great faith. He raised a person from the dead, healed people, and saw God do amazing things. It is evident that once Paul was converted, he lived a righteous life. So did he suffer? Yes! This passage lists many of the ways that he suffered. *2 Corinthians 6:3-10 (NIV) ³ We put no stumbling block in anyone's path, so that our ministry will not be discredited. ⁴ Rather, as servants of God we commend ourselves in every way: in great endurance; in troubles, hardships and distresses; ⁵ in beatings, imprisonments and riots; in hard work, sleepless nights and hunger; ⁶ in purity, understanding, patience and kindness; in the Holy Spirit and in sincere love; ⁷ in truthful speech and in the power of God; with weapons of righteousness in the right hand and in the left; ⁸ through glory and dishonor, bad report and good report; genuine, yet regarded as impostors; ⁹ known, yet regarded as unknown; dying, and yet we live on; beaten, and yet not killed; ¹⁰ sorrowful, yet always rejoicing; poor, yet making many rich; having nothing, and yet possessing everything.*

Paul said that he had weapons of righteousness in the right hand and in the left hand. He was bold and confident in his relationship with Christ. He was ready to admit that he was on a different team. He was ready to tell the world which side was going to win in the end.

Are we willing to be on the right team and wear our team's colors in public? We are to clothe ourselves with Christ. We need to stand up for Christ at home, at work, and in our communities. We need to embrace Him and teach others to do the same. Satan hates Christ. When we speak, act, and love like Christ, his opposing team will persecute us. We need to be ready and willing to be persecuted.

Conclusion

We may suffer because of persecutions. We may suffer because God is molding us. We may suffer because of natural causes and the effects of sin in this world. But no matter why we suffer, we can trust in God.

Peter says it this way in *1 Peter 1:5-7 (NIV)* *[5] ... the salvation that is ready to be revealed in the last time. [6] In this you greatly rejoice, though now for a little while you may have had to suffer grief in all kinds of trials. [7] These have come so that your faith—of greater worth than gold, which perishes even though refined by fire—may be proved genuine and may result in praise, glory and honor when Jesus Christ is revealed.*

These have come so that your faith may be proved genuine. Can you rejoice in your suffering and be glad that God is molding you into His image? He loves you enough to discipline you and prepare you for His kingdom! Thank you, Lord, for my suffering!

Paul says this in *Romans 5:2-5 (NIV)* *[2] ...And we rejoice in the hope of the glory of God. [3] Not only so, but we also rejoice in our sufferings, because we know that suffering produces perseverance; ⁴ perseverance, character; and character, hope.⁵ And hope does not disappoint us, because God has poured out his love into our hearts by the Holy Spirit, whom he has given us.*

2 Thessalonians 1:4-5 (NIV) ⁴ Therefore, among God's churches we boast about your perseverance and faith in all the persecutions and trials you are enduring. ⁵ All this is evidence that God's judgment is right, and as a result you will be counted worthy of the kingdom of God, **for which you are suffering.**

We may wonder *why* and never understand *why*, but we can trust that God knows *why*. He is a loving God who is full of compassion and mercy. James 5:10-11 (NIV) ¹⁰ Brothers, **as an example of patience in the face of suffering**, take the prophets who spoke in the name of the Lord. ¹¹ As you know, **we consider blessed those who have persevered**. You have heard of Job's perseverance and have seen what the Lord finally brought about. The Lord is full of compassion and mercy.

When we begin to question why a loving God would allow good people to suffer, we need to remember that we are not good people. We deserve to suffer because we have sinned. We have broken God's law and deserve the just punishments of our sin.

The fate of sin eventually leads to death, an eternal separation from God in hell. People who ask why a loving God allows suffering need to remember how Jesus suffered for us. The influential Archbishop of Canterbury, William Temple, once put it like this: *"There cannot be a God of love," people say, "because if there was, and he looked upon the world, his heart would break." The church points to the Cross and says, "It did break."* Christ came and suffered our punishment so that we would not have to spend an eternity in hell. We suffer on this earth because of our own sin and the sins of others. We deserve it. God came to redeem us and to spare us from an eternity of suffering.

Hebrews 2:10-11 (NIV) [10] In bringing many sons to glory, it was fitting that God, for whom and through whom everything exists, should make the author of their salvation perfect through suffering. [11] Both the one who makes men holy and those who are made holy are of the same family. So Jesus is not ashamed to call them brothers.

How amazing and great is God's love for us! The God who gave us the freedom of choice, now takes upon himself the consequences for our wrong choices.

Hebrews 2:9 (NIV) [9] But we see Jesus, who was made a little lower than the angels, now crowned with glory and honor because he suffered death, so that by the grace of God he might taste death for everyone.

God offers us the choice to repent, to make Him Lord, and to live in His kingdom forever; a kingdom with no more suffering, no more crying, and no more pain.

WORKSHEET FOR CHURCH GOVERNMENT
LIFE TRUTH # 9
THE CHURCH SUFFERS FOR CHRIST

Question: How should the church view suffering?
Answer: God uses sufferings to mold us. We will suffer for Christ on this earth.

Philippians 1:29 (NIV) *²⁹ For it has been granted to you on behalf of Christ not only to believe on him, but also to suffer for him,*

> Write out the Life Truth, question, and answer on one side of an index card and the verse on the other side. Keep it in your Bible for the week. Work on it every day individually and as a family. Have it memorized by next week.

Read Philippians 1:29. What two things have been granted to us?

What do you think it means when it says that we have been granted to suffer for Christ?

Read Deuteronomy 8:2,3. Why did God allow them to suffer in these ways?

Read John 9:1-3. Why was this man suffering?

Read Romans 5:1-5. What does suffering produce?

What does perseverance produce?
What does character produce?

Read Romans 8:18. How can this verse comfort those who are suffering?

Read Romans 8:28. What does this verse reveal to us about God allowing us to suffer?

Read 1 Peter 4:1, 2. He who has suffered is done with what?   Why?

Read 1 Peter 4:12-19. What are we to do when we suffer for Christ?   What is the difference between suffering as a Christian and suffering for disobedience?
Judgment is to begin where? (v17)
When we suffer for the name of Christ what does that reveal about us?

Read Philippians 3:10, 11. What is the fellowship of sharing in Christ sufferings?

Read 2 Cor. 12:7-10. Why did God allow Paul to suffer in this way?
What word did Paul use to describe the suffering?

Based on this LIFE TRUTH, what can you do individually and as a family to better understand suffering? How can you share in the sufferings of Christ?

CHURCH-GOVERNMENT LIFE TRUTH # 10
THE CHURCH PREPARES FOR CHRIST'S RETURN

I used the illustration of a sports fanatic, attending a game in the opposing team's stadium, in our last Life Truth. His attire, banners, and cheers for the opposing team were sure to get him persecuted. Hopefully, this illustration helps you visualize how Christians, being clothed in Christ, may face persecution living in the opposing team's territory on this earth.

Paul speaks of these opposing sides in *Philippians 1:20-30 (NIV)* [20] *I eagerly expect and hope that I will in no way be ashamed, but will have sufficient courage so that now as always Christ will be exalted in my body, whether by life or by death.* [21] *For to me, to live is Christ and to die is gain.* [22] *If I am to go on living in the body, this will mean fruitful labor for me. Yet what shall I choose? I do not know!* [23] *I am torn between the two: I desire to depart and be with Christ, which is better by far;* [24] *but it is more necessary for you that I remain in the body.* [25] *Convinced of this, I know that I will remain, and I will continue with all of you for your progress and joy in the faith,* [26] *so that through my being with you again your joy in Christ Jesus will overflow on account of me.*

Paul said, "*to live is Christ and to die is gain.*" Why would Paul say that to die is gain? Does death equal gain? As Christians, we understand that this life is not all there is. We know there is an eternal life after this one. When God created us in his image, he offered us eternity. But eternity exists in two places. There will be those who followed Christ and those who did not. Those who followed Christ will go to heaven with Jesus forever. Those who chose not to follow Christ will spend an eternity in hell.

Paul remained in the opposing team's territory so he could persuade others to get on the winning team even though it was his desire to be done with this sinful world, its persecutions, and its sufferings. He exhorts the Christians in Philippi to be brave; to put on their team's clothing and face the persecution that is ahead. *[27] Whatever happens, conduct yourselves in a manner worthy of the gospel of Christ. Then, whether I come and see you or only hear about you in my absence, I will know that you stand firm in one spirit, contending as one man for the faith of the gospel [28] without being frightened in any way by those who oppose you. This is a sign to them that they will be destroyed, but that you will be saved—and that by God. [29] For it has been granted to you on behalf of Christ not only to believe on him, but also to suffer for him, [30] since you are going through the same struggle you saw I had, and now hear that I still have.*

The opposing team will suffer for all eternity, but what will happen to the Christians? What is our fate? Jesus told the disciples in *John 14:1-3 (NIV) [1] "Do not let your hearts be troubled. Trust in God; trust also in me. [2] In my Father's house are many rooms; if it were not so,*

I would have told you. I am going there to prepare a place for you. ³ **And if I go and prepare a place for you, I will come back and take you to be with me that you also may be where I am.**

Hebrews 9:28 (NIV) ²⁸ *so Christ was sacrificed once to take away the sins of many people; and he will appear a second time, not to bear sin, but to bring salvation to those who are waiting for him.*

Christ will return to bring salvation to those who are waiting for him.

Paul addresses the church of Corinth in *I Corinthians 2:9 (NIV)* ⁹ *However, as it is written: "No eye has seen, no ear has heard, no mind has conceived what God has prepared for those who love him"*—Our minds cannot even conceive how awesome heaven is going to be!

Even the Old Testament prophets spoke about such a day when God would bring us into heaven. *Isaiah 65:17-19 (NIV)* ¹⁷ *"Behold, I will create new heavens and a new earth. The former things will not be remembered, nor will they come to mind.* ¹⁸ *But be glad and rejoice forever in what I will create, for I will create Jerusalem to be a delight and its people a joy.* ¹⁹ *I will rejoice over Jerusalem and take delight in my people; the sound of weeping and of crying will be heard in it no more.*

Although we cannot comprehend all that eternity is going to be, God did give us some details about it.

1. Eternity is forever

The word eternity means eternal or everlasting. The place we enter when we die, or when Christ returns, will be our fate for all eternity. **Our future home, whether heaven or hell, will be forever.**

Revelation 20:10 (NIV) [10] And the devil, who deceived them, was thrown into the lake of burning sulfur, where the beast and the false prophet had been thrown. They will be tormented day and night for ever and ever.

Matthew 25:46 (NIV) [46] "Then they will go away to eternal punishment, but the righteous to eternal life." This passage reveals not only that the wicked will go away to eternal punishment but that the righteous will go away to eternal life. There are other passages that reveal to us that heaven will be forever.

John 3:16 (NIV) [16] "For God so loved the world that he gave his one and only Son, that whoever believes in him shall not perish but have eternal life.

John 5:24 (NIV) [24] "I tell you the truth, whoever hears my word and believes him who sent me has eternal life and will not be condemned; he has crossed over from death to life.

2. Hell is constant suffering and Heaven is exempt from suffering

We have already looked at a few passages that refer to the constant suffering the people in hell will endure for eternity. This suffering is the fate of those who have chosen to reject Christ's offer of salvation from their sin.

The prophet Isaiah and the book of Revelation both speak of heaven as a place free from suffering. *Revelation 21:3-4 (NIV) [3] And I heard a loud voice from the throne saying, "Now the dwelling of God is with men, and he will live with them. They will be his people, and God himself will be with them and be their God. [4] He will wipe every tear from their eyes. There will be no more death or mourning or crying or pain, for the old order of things has passed away."*

There will be no more suffering in heaven because the curse of sin will be done away with. Sin is what brings decay, suffering, and death. No more sin means that it is a home of righteousness. A place free from death, mourning, crying, or pain! Can you imagine? No more pain! No more suffering! This is why Paul said, *"to live is Christ and to die is gain."*

The church is told repeatedly in the New Testament to focus on heaven. Our goal is to be in heaven with Jesus forever. We are to prepare for Christ's return, knowing that any day may be our last one upon this earth.

Here are some Scriptural principles to help us prepare for the return of Christ:

1. Keep your eyes on the heavenly city

In Hebrews, Chapter 11, it speaks about great people of faith. It mentions the faith of Abraham and his heavenly focus. It says in *Hebrews 11:10-16 (NIV)* *¹⁰ For he was looking forward to the city with foundations, whose architect and builder is God.*

Abraham, even though God blessed him with great wealth, had his eyes on the heavenly city and not his earthly possessions.

In the book of Genesis, we get a glimpse of Abraham's focus. As Abraham and his nephew's herds grew, they became too large for them to stay together. Abraham decided to split up and part ways. Abraham, being the elder, could have chosen which direction he would go, sending Lot in the opposite direction. Instead, he allowed Lot to choose first. *Genesis 13:6-18 (NIV) ⁶ But the land could not support them while they stayed together, for their possessions were so great that they were not able to stay together. ⁷ And quarreling arose between Abram's herdsmen and the herdsmen of Lot. The Canaanites and Perizzites were also living in the land at that time. ⁸ So Abram said to Lot, "Let's not have any quarreling between you and me, or between your herdsmen and mine, for we are brothers. ⁹ Is not the whole land before you? Let's part company. If you go to the left, I'll go to the right; if you go to the right, I'll go to the left."* ¹⁰ *Lot looked up and saw that the whole plain of the Jordan was well watered, like the garden of the LORD, like the land of Egypt, toward Zoar. (This was before the LORD destroyed Sodom and Gomorrah.)* ¹¹ *So Lot chose for himself the whole plain of the Jordan and set out toward the east. The two men parted company:* ¹² *Abram lived in the land of Canaan, while Lot lived among the cities of the plain and pitched his tents near Sodom.* ¹³ *Now the men of Sodom were wicked and were sinning greatly against the LORD.* ¹⁴ *The LORD said to Abram after Lot had parted from him, "Lift up your eyes from where you are and look north and south, east and west.* ¹⁵ *All the land that you see I will give to you and your offspring forever.* ¹⁶ *I will make your offspring like the dust of the earth, so that if anyone could count the dust, then your offspring could be counted.* ¹⁷ *Go, walk through the length and breadth of the land, for I am giving it to you."* ¹⁸ *So Abram moved his tents and went to live near the great trees of Mamre at Hebron, where he built an altar to the LORD.*

Lot chose to go where his focus was; his earthly wealth. His decision caused him to move near an immoral place. Eventually, he moved to the immoral city of Sodom seeking even more wealth. His lack of focus on heaven caused him and his daughters to make great compromises. It also caused them to lose all that they had.

Abraham's focus remained upon the heavenly city. Even though he was blessed with earthly things, he did not change his focus. Paul tells us to be satisfied whether we have plenty or we are in want. Christians must keep their eyes on heaven; not on the material things of this world. Homes, cars, televisions, clothing, jewelry, etc., will not mean anything when the Lord returns or Christ calls us home. Paul said, *"we brought nothing into this world and we will take nothing out."* I'm sure Lot had a whole new perspective on life when he left Sodom with nothing.

Hebrews, Chapter 11, tells us that the great people of faith had this Biblical perspective of keeping their eyes on the heavenly city. *[13] All these people were still living by faith when they died. They did not receive the things promised; they only saw them and welcomed them from a distance. And they admitted that they were aliens and strangers on earth. [14] People who say such things show that they are looking for a country of their own. [15] If they had been thinking of the country they had left, they would have had opportunity to return. [16] Instead, they were longing for a better country—a heavenly one. Therefore God is not ashamed to be called their God, for he has prepared a city for them.*

God gives us free will that allows us to go the wrong way and become consumed with the things of this world. It is one of the dangers that Jesus reminds us of in the parable of the sower. *Matthew 13:22 (NIV) [22] The one who received the seed that fell among the thorns is the man who hears the word, but the worries of this life and the deceitfulness of wealth choke it, making it unfruitful.* The deceitfulness of wealth can choke us to death. Great people of faith turn away from greed and covetousness and remain focused on the heavenly city.

A proper focus will cause us to share Christ with a greater fervor. It will help us to realize it is more blessed to give than to receive. It will cause us to give more to others and not be consumed with our own selfish wants. When we stand before God one day, He will say *well done* to those who generously cared about the needs of others.

2. Scoffers will come to discredit the return of Christ

Someday, this earth will be destroyed. God is going to make a new heaven and a new earth that is free of sin. Peter talks about what it will be like when this day comes. He reveals to us that scoffers will come and try to discredit the return of Christ.

2 Peter 3:3-13 (NIV) [3] First of all, you must understand that in the last days scoffers will come, scoffing and following their own evil desires. [4] They will say, "Where is this 'coming' he promised? Ever since our fathers died, everything goes on as it has since the beginning of creation." [5] But they deliberately forget that long ago by God's word the heavens existed and the earth was formed out of water and by water. [6] By these waters also the world of that time was deluged and destroyed.
[7] By the same word the present heavens and earth are reserved for fire, being kept for the day of judgment and destruction of ungodly men. [8] But do not forget this one

thing, dear friends: With the Lord a day is like a thousand years, and a thousand years are like a day. [9] The Lord is not slow in keeping his promise, as some understand slowness. He is patient with you, not wanting anyone to perish, but everyone to come to repentance. [10] But the day of the Lord will come like a thief. The heavens will disappear with a roar; the elements will be destroyed by fire, and the earth and everything in it will be laid bare. [11] Since everything will be destroyed in this way, what kind of people ought you to be? You ought to live holy and godly lives [12] as you look forward to the day of God and speed its coming. That day will bring about the destruction of the heavens by fire, and the elements will melt in the heat. [13] But in keeping with his promise we are looking forward to a new heaven and a new earth, the home of righteousness.

Peter reminds us and the scoffers, that God devastated the earth with a flood because of man's sin, and He has set a day to do it again. It will be on the Day of Judgment when Christ returns. The reason it seems to be taking so long is because of God's patience and love for man. He doesn't desire for anyone to perish. But don't mistake his patience for a lack of zeal to punish the wicked. He will judge justly. For those who have not repented of their sins, the day of the Lord will be a day of terror.

Peter asks the question, "Since everything will be destroyed this way what kind of people ought you to be?" Then he answers his own question, "we ought to live holy and godly lives as we look forward to the day of God *and speed its coming."* Christians need to realize that people are going to scoff and mock the coming of the Lord. They will live sinful lives filled with all kinds of passions. We must keep our heads and our hearts focused upon Christ's return. We do not want to be doing anything that would shame Christ, especially when He returns.

Paul writes to the Church in Thessalonica and reminds them that the day will come like a thief in the night. *I Thessalonians 5:1-11 (NIV) ¹ Now, brothers, about times and dates we do not need to write to you, ² for you know very well that the day of the Lord will come like a thief in the night. ³ While people are saying, "Peace and safety," destruction will come on them suddenly, as labor pains on a pregnant woman, and they will not escape. ⁴ But you, brothers, are not in darkness so that this day should surprise you like a thief. ⁵ You are all sons of the light and sons of the day. We do not belong to the night or to the darkness. ⁶ So then, let us not be like others, who are asleep, but let us be alert and self-controlled. ⁷ For those who sleep, sleep at night, and those who get drunk, get drunk at night. ⁸ But since we belong to the day, let us be self-controlled, putting on faith and love as a breastplate, and the hope of salvation as a helmet. ⁹ For God did not appoint us to suffer wrath but to receive salvation through our Lord Jesus Christ. ¹⁰ He died for us so that, whether we are awake or asleep, we may live together with him. ¹¹ Therefore encourage one another and build each other up, just as in fact you are doing.*

Since the return could be at any time, we need to be self-controlled and alert. We need to be prepared for the Lord's return and ready to welcome the groom. The church is called the bride of Christ. If a groom showed up for his wedding, and his bride was not dressed and ready, it would be a disgrace. The bride would be disrespecting her husband and treating him with contempt. Those that are not ready for the wedding will suffer wrath, but those who prepare themselves for the wedding day, will gain eternal life. Don't listen to the mockers and scoffers. Instead meditate upon God's Word and trust in His promises that He will return.

3. Remind each other about Christ's return

Paul wrote to Titus about the grace of God that brings salvation in *Titus 2:11-14 (NIV)* [11] *For the grace of God that brings salvation has appeared to all men.* [12] *It teaches us to say "No" to ungodliness and worldly passions, and to live self-controlled, upright and godly lives in this present age,* [13] *while we wait for the blessed hope--the glorious appearing of our great God and Savior, Jesus Christ,* [14] *who gave himself for us to redeem us from all wickedness and to purify for himself a people that are his very own, eager to do what is good.*

God's grace helps us to prepare for the wedding day and stay away from sin. Sin is like getting grass stains and dirt all over our wedding dress. God's grace empowers us to clean it and keep it clean. Paul uses the phrase, *"while we wait for the blessed hope."*

Blessed hope refers to *"the glorious appearing of our great God and Savior, Jesus Christ."* We are to be encouraging each other and reminding one another about Christ's return. This is our *blessed hope*. It gives us courage and strength to walk in righteousness. It is why we can deny ourselves of this world's sinful passions.

The Greek meaning of the word *hope* is deeper than the American meaning. A flippant, *"I hope this happens,"* is the American meaning of hope. The Greek meaning of the word *hope* is a certainty. *Hope* means there is **no doubt** that Christ will return. It is this "*blessed hope*" that helps believers stay on the straight and narrow.

The church in Thessalonica was concerned that the loved ones who were dead and buried would miss out on the return of Christ. Paul encouraged them that we will all see Jesus on His return; those that have died and those who are still alive. Paul uses the term "fall asleep" to refer to the ones who have died. This term also reminds us that Christians will not die, but will have eternal life.

1 Thessalonians 4:13-18 (NIV) [13] Brothers, we do not want you to be ignorant about those who fall asleep, or to grieve like the rest of men, who have no hope. [14] We believe that Jesus died and rose again and so we believe that God will bring with Jesus those who have fallen asleep in him. [15] According to the Lord's own word, we tell you that we who are still alive, who are left till the coming of the Lord, will certainly not precede those who have fallen asleep. ⁱ⁶ For the Lord himself will come down from heaven, with a loud command, with the voice of the archangel and with the trumpet call of God, and the dead in Christ will rise first. ⁱ⁷ After that, we who are still alive and are left will be caught up together with them in the clouds to meet the Lord in the air. And so we will be with the Lord forever. ⁱ⁸ Therefore **encourage each other with these words.**

Paul gives us a glimpse of what will happen when Christ returns. The graves will open up and the dead in Christ will rise first. When Christ died on the cross, He performed a similar miracle. It is recorded in *Matthew 27:52-53 (NIV) ⁵² The tombs broke open and the bodies of many holy people who had died were raised to life. ⁵³ They came out of the tombs, and after Jesus' resurrection they went into the holy city and appeared to many people.*

4. Always be ready

There are many passages that refer to the return of Christ. These passages should comfort us and remind us to encourage one another to press on. Don't lose your focus or your hope. Prepare for the wedding banquet because the groom is coming. As the writer of Hebrews says in *Hebrews 10:37 (NIV) ³⁷ For in just a very little while, He who is coming will come and will not delay.*

Jesus told his disciples to be ready. His return could happen at any hour. He also warned them that it would be like the time of Noah and Lot. In Noah's day, the people were eating and drinking. They were not concerned about the coming judgment. The flood came and destroyed them all. In Lot's day, the people were immoral and were not concerned about the coming judgment. Burning sulfur rained down on them from heaven. Jesus says that, The Day of the Lord, which is the Second Coming, will be the same. People will be unprepared. Luke 17:24-36 (NIV)

24 For the Son of Man in his day will be like the lightning, which flashes and lights up the sky from one end to the other. 25 But first he must suffer many things and be rejected by this generation. 26 "Just as it was in the days of Noah, so also will it be in the days of the Son of Man. 27 People were eating, drinking, marrying and being given in marriage up to the day Noah entered the ark. Then the flood came and destroyed them all. 28 "It was the same in the days of Lot. People were eating and drinking, buying and selling, planting and building. 29 But the day Lot left Sodom, fire and sulfur rained down from heaven and destroyed them all. 30 "It will be just like this on the day the Son of Man is revealed. 31 On that day no one who is on the roof of his house, with his goods inside, should go down to get them. Likewise, no one in the field should go back for anything. 32 Remember Lot's wife! 33 Whoever tries to keep his life will lose it, and whoever loses his life will preserve it.

What will the return of Christ look like?

We already know that when Christ returns, the dead in Christ will come out of their graves first. Those who are still alive will be caught up together with them in the clouds and meet the Lord in the air. As the disciples were watching Christ ascend into heaven, the angels appeared and said in, *Acts 1:11 (NIV)* *¹¹ "Men of Galilee," they said, "why do you stand here looking into the sky? This same Jesus, who has been taken from you into heaven, will come back in the same way you have seen him go into heaven."*

Jesus warns His disciples to be ready because the times will be like those of Noah and Lot. He lets them know that some will be taken and others will be left. *Luke 17:34-35 (NIV) ³⁴ I tell you, on that night two people will be in one bed; one will be taken and the other left. ³⁵ Two women will be grinding grain together; one will be taken and the other left.*

Christ will return. Everyone will see Him at the same time. He will appear in the sky. John gives us more insight into His return in, *Revelation 19:11-16 (NIV) ¹¹ I saw heaven standing open and there before me was a white horse, whose rider is called Faithful and True. With justice he judges and makes war. ¹² His eyes are like blazing fire, and on his head are many crowns. He has a name written on him that no one knows but he himself. ¹³ He is dressed in a robe dipped in blood, and his name is the Word of God. ¹⁴ The armies of heaven were following him, riding on white horses and dressed in fine linen, white and clean. ¹⁵ Out of his mouth comes a sharp sword with which to strike down the nations. "He will rule them with an iron scepter." He treads the winepress of the fury of the wrath of God Almighty. [16] On his robe and on his thigh he has this name written: KING OF KINGS AND LORD OF LORDS.*

What an awesome sight it will be when Christ returns! Those that have accepted Christ will rejoice, while those that have rejected Him will mourn. God's wrath and fury will be poured out when He returns. Those who are not ready will experience it.

The book of Matthew reveals even more about His return. Matthew 24:30-31 (NIV) [30] "At that time the sign of the Son of Man will appear in the sky, and all the nations of the earth will mourn. They will see the Son of Man coming on the clouds of the sky, with power and great glory. [31] And he will send his angels with a loud trumpet call, and they will gather his elect from the four winds, from one end of the heavens to the other.

As the dead rise and we begin to meet them in the air, the angels will be gathering the elect together. The elect are those that have repented and made Jesus the Lord of their lives. Again the passage points out that the nations of the earth will mourn. Revelations speaks of the mourning and the fact that every eye will see Him. *Revelation 1:7 (NIV) [7] Look, he is coming with the clouds, and every eye will see him, even those who pierced him; and all the peoples of the earth will mourn because of him. So shall it be! Amen.*

Will Christ's return be a time of rejoicing or a time of mourning for you? It all depends upon your preparations now. Will you live the rest of your days to glorify God? Will you live everyday as if it is the day Christ will return? If you choose to put off getting ready for His return, the day will be one of wrath and fury for you.

No one knows the day or the hour. It will come like a thief in the night. If you have hidden sin in your life, now is the time to make it right! Today is the day of salvation. Choose Christ before it is too late. Don't think you have days to prepare; tomorrow will come and it will be the day of the Lord. Paul tells the church of Corinth that it will happen in a flash. It will happen so quickly that you will not have time to get ready. *I Corinthians 15:51-52 (NIV) [51] Listen, I tell you a mystery: We will not all sleep, but we will all be changed— [52] in a flash, in the twinkling of an eye, at the last trumpet. For the trumpet will sound, the dead will be raised imperishable, and we will be changed.*

Jesus gives us some warning about when the Day will come. The disciples asked Him, *"What will the sign be of your coming?" Matthew 24:3-8 (NIV) [3] As Jesus was sitting on the Mount of Olives, the disciples came to him privately. "Tell us," they said, "when will this happen, and what will be the sign of your coming and of the end of the age?" [4] Jesus answered: "Watch out that no one deceives you. [5] For many will come in my name, claiming, 'I am the Christ,' and will deceive many. [6] You will hear of wars and rumors of wars, but see to it that you are not alarmed. Such things must happen, but the end is still to come. ⁷ Nation will rise against nation, and kingdom against kingdom. There will be famines and earthquakes in various places. ⁸ All these are the beginning of birth pains.*

We are seeing these things all around us in our generation. Are we ready?

Are you prepared for the return of Christ? Have you repented of your sins and made Jesus the Lord of your life? If not, do it now and don't delay! Tell everyone you know to always be ready. *Matthew 24:44 (NIV) ⁴⁴ So you also must be ready, because the Son of Man will come at an hour when you do not expect him.*

The very last verses in the Bible say this in *Revelation 22:20-21 (NIV) ²⁰ He who testifies to these things says, "Yes, I am coming soon." Amen. Come, Lord Jesus. ²¹ The grace of the Lord Jesus be with God's people. Amen.*

WORKSHEET FOR CHURCH GOVERNMENT
LIFE TRUTH #10
THE CHURCH PREPARES FOR CHRIST'S RETURN

Question: How should the church prepare for Christ's return?

Answer: The church should always be ready for no one knows the day or the hour of Christ's return.

Matthew 24:44 (NIV) 44 So you also must be ready, because the Son of Man will come at an hour when you do not expect him.

> Write out the Life Truth, question, and answer on one side of an index card and the verse on the other side. Keep it in your Bible for the week. Work on it every day individually and as a family. Have it memorized by next week.

Read Matthew 24:36-51. Who is the only one who knows the day and the hour of Christ's return?

What was it like during the days of Noah?

Where will the person go who is taken? (v40,41)

How can we be ready for the return of Christ?

What will happen to those who are not ready?

Read Mark 13:32-37. What kinds of things might a person be doing who is "sleeping" when Christ returns?

Read Matthew 25:1-13. Who do the ten virgins represent?

What happened to the foolish virgins?

Read Matthew 24:3-35. What will people claim? (v5)

How will we know when Christ's returns? (v27)

What are some of the signs that will happen before Christ's coming?

What does the phrase "turn away from the faith" mean? (v10)

What will grow cold? What will that look like in society?

What will false prophets be able to do? (24)

Based on this LIFE TRUTH what can you do individually and as a family to prepare for Christ's return? How can you help be prepared for the return of Christ?